Collins
My First
World Atlas

Collins My First World Atlas

Collins
An imprint of HarperCollins Publishers
Westerhill Road
Bishopbriggs
Glasgow G64 2QT

© HarperCollins Publishers 2013
Maps © Collins Bartholomew Ltd 2011

First published 2011
Reprinted 2012
Second edition 2013

ISBN 978-0-00-752126-5

Imp 001

The contents of this edition of Collins My First
World Atlas are believed correct at the time of
printing. Nevertheless the publishers can accept
no responsibility for errors or omissions, changes
in the detail given, or for any expense or loss
thereby caused.

British Library Cataloguing in Publication Data
A catalogue record for this book is available from
the British Library.

Printed and bound by South China Printing
Company, China

All mapping in this atlas is generated from Collins
Bartholomew digital databases.
Collins Bartholomew, the UK's leading independent
geographical information supplier, can provide a
digital, custom, and premium mapping service to
a variety of markets.
For further information:
Tel: +44 (0) 141 306 3752
e-mail: collinsbartholomew@harpercollins.co.uk

Visit our websites at:
www.harpercollins.co.uk
www.collinsbartholomew.com
www.collinsmaps.com

Cover and title image © YadvigaGr/Shutterstock.com

Contents

How to use the atlas

Take a journey around the world with this atlas. It is divided up into continents, regions and countries. Each map is full of small picture symbols which will introduce you to the lifestyle of people, wildlife and interesting places found in far off lands.

World maps

The introductory pages show maps of the whole world and from these you can find the regions with the most interesting features. You can find out more about these by searching through the continents and regions mapped in the rest of the atlas. At the bottom of each World page is a list of symbols used on pages within the atlas. Try to find the countries where the symbols are shown then look at the other interesting features found in that country.

Below the world map each 'Did you know? lists some fascinating facts and statistics.

Did you know?

- Only 12 people have ever walked on the moon.
- A spacecraft takes 3 days to travel from earth to the moon.

World

The world is full of interesting places. Many countries have famous buildings like castles, churches and palaces and some of these are named on the map.

Arctic

NORTH AMERICA

Seattle Space Needle

Statue of Liberty

Edinburgh Castle

EUROPE

Eiffel Tower

Kennedy Space Center

Colosseum

Mexican pyramid

Atlantic Ocean

Pacific Ocean

SOUTH AMERICA

Did you know?

- Only 12 people have ever walked on the moon.
- A spacecraft takes 3 days to travel from earth to the moon.

Statue de Jesus

Did you know?

- The Eiffel tower is over 300 metres (984 feet) high.
- There are 1660 steps from the foot of the tower to the top.
- In summer, the tower is 15 centimetres (6 inches) taller because of the warmer weather.

Look through the maps in this atlas to find the other places shown below.
▼

Arc de Triomphe

Golden Temple, Amritsar

terracotta soldier

Dome of the Rock

vi

Maps of each continent

How well do you know the flags of the world? Turn to the map of a continent and every flag will be shown beside its country. In addition all the statistics about the continent are listed. These include its highest mountain, longest river, biggest country and much more.

On every spread of a continent there is also a short activity which relates to the information shown on the map.

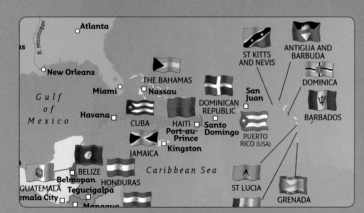

R. Mississippi

Atlanta

New Orleans

THE BAHAMAS

Miami

Nassau

Gulf of Mexico

Havana

CUBA

HAITI Port-au-Prince

Kingston

JAMAICA

DOMINICAN REPUBLIC

Santo Domingo

San Juan

PUERTO RICO (USA)

ST KITTS AND NEVIS

ANTIGUA AND BARBUDA

DOMINICA

BARBADOS

Caribbean Sea

ST LUCIA

GRENADA

BELIZE

Belmopan

HONDURAS

Tegucigalpa

GUATEMALA

emala City

Managua

Maps of regions and countries

Imagine you have just arrived in a new country. What will it be like? What do you want to do or see here?

The symbols placed on the countries can help you to decide. Look at the symbols in the neighbouring countries and plan a journey right across the region. There is so much to see and do.

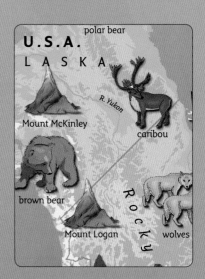

Watch a Sumo wrestling match!
Take a train journey!

Go walking in the mountains!
See lots of animals!

Find out more from the facts placed around the maps.

It's a fact

Each year a panda can eat 5 tonnes of bamboo.

It's a fact

Ice hockey is one of Canada's most popular sports.

Try the activity found at the bottom of each map.

This will let you know just how much you have learnt from the map. All the answers are listed at the back of the atlas.

Try this!
China has many different animals. Look at the map and find

The big furry animal who loves to eat bamboo.

Many sports are played in Japan

Can you name 2 of these?

Try this!
Canada has many different animals and birds. Look at the map and find

4 types of bird
2 types of dog
3 furry wild animals

Where have you been?

You may like to see what other children think of the places they have visited or lived in. On pages 48–51 you can read some of the comments we have gathered from children. Have you been to the same places? What comment would you make about the places you have visited?

Kenya
We were in a big car and saw elephants and lions. I liked the lions but they had big teeth. It was very dusty and hot.
Katie

USA
I like Universal Studio because it has fantastic rides. I would give it a ten out of ten.
Sam

Index

You may know the name of a place you would like to visit but can't find the map it appears on. Turn to the index and find the name. The index will tell you which page in the atlas to turn to and where the place is on the map.

World

The world is full of interesting places. Many countries have famous buildings like castles, churches and palaces and some of these are named on the map.

Arctic

NORTH AMERICA

Seattle Space Needle

Statue of Liberty

Kennedy Space Center

Mexican pyramid

Edinburgh Castle

EUROPE

Eiffel Tower

Colosseum

Atlantic Ocean

Pacific Ocean

SOUTH AMERICA

Statue de Jesus

A

Did you know?

- Only 12 people have ever walked on the moon.
- A spacecraft takes 3 days to travel from earth to the moon.

Did you know?

- The Eiffel tower is over 300 metres (984 feet) high.
- There are 1660 steps from the foot of the tower to the top.
- In summer, the tower is 15 centimetres (6 inches) taller because of the warmer weather.

Look through the maps in this atlas to find the other places shown below.

▼

Arc de Triomphe

Golden Temple, Amritsar

terracotta soldier

Dome of the Rock

Interesting places

_e a n_

Kremlin

_A S I A_

Pacific

Ocean

Great Wall of China

Sphinx

Taj Mahal

_I C A_

Indian

Ocean

Did you know?

_O C E A N I A_

ulu house

- The Great Wall of China is the longest wall in the world.
- It winds up and down mountains and across fields and deserts.
- The wall is as tall as 2 double decker buses.

Sydney Opera House

Chilean chapel

Big Ben

Berber architecture

Angkor Wat

World

Animals and birds live all over the world. Each have their favourite places to live. This may depend on the climate and vegetation of the country in which they are found.

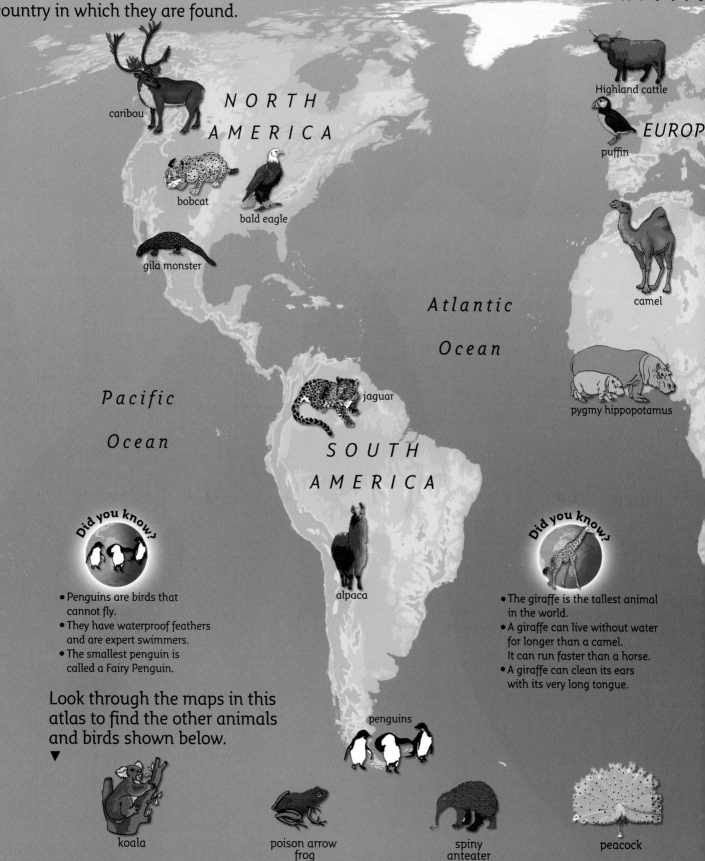

Arctic

Highland cattle

EUROP

puffin

camel

Atlantic

Ocean

pygmy hippopotamus

caribou

NORTH
AMERICA

bobcat

bald eagle

gila monster

Pacific

Ocean

jaguar

SOUTH
AMERICA

alpaca

Did you know?

- Penguins are birds that cannot fly.
- They have waterproof feathers and are expert swimmers.
- The smallest penguin is called a Fairy Penguin.

Did you know?

- The giraffe is the tallest animal in the world.
- A giraffe can live without water for longer than a camel. It can run faster than a horse.
- A giraffe can clean its ears with its very long tongue.

penguins

Look through the maps in this atlas to find the other animals and birds shown below.
▼

koala

poison arrow frog

spiny anteater

peacock

Animals and Birds

cean

lynx

Siberian tiger

brown bear

ASIA

Pacific

Ocean

giraffe

giant panda

gorilla

Indian

Ocean

RICA

Did you know?

- A panda is a type of bear. It can climb trees.
- A baby panda is smaller than a mouse.
- Pandas eat for up to 16 hours every day.

zebra

OCEANIA

kangaroo

kiwi

alligator

skunk

yak

snow goose

World

Different types of food are grown and eaten all over the world. This map of the world shows where some of our favourite foods are grown.

Arctic

NORTH AMERICA

cheese

EUROPE

apples

cranberries

peanuts

pizza

hamburgers

dates

Atlantic

Ocean

Pacific

Ocean

oranges

bananas

A

SOUTH AMERICA

Did you know?

- Apples can be red, green or yellow.
- One apple tree can produce 400 apples every year.
- Apples can be as small as a cherry, or as large as a grapefruit.

grapes

Did you know?

- A coconut can float on the water.
- Coconuts are grown in half the countries in the world.
- You can drink coconut juice. It is the liquid found inside a coconut.

Look through the maps in this atlas to find the other foods shown below.

▼

tortilla

pumpkin pie

croissants

almonds

x

Food and Drink

e a n

potatoes

wheat

kebabs

A S I A

Pacific

Ocean

bowl of rice

I C A

tea

pineapples

Indian

Ocean

coconuts

Did you know?

- Over half the people in the world eat rice every day.
- In China the word for rice is the same as the word for food.
- Rice is a type of grass.

rapes

seafood

O C E A N I A

kiwi fruit

spaghetti

olives

wheat

sardines

World

People play sport all over the world. Popular sports, like football, are played in almost every country. Different sports are shown on the map.

Arctic

NORTH AMERICA

snow boarding

cricket

EUROPE

ice hockey

rugby

bull fighting

American football

football

Atlantic

Ocean

Pacific

Ocean

SOUTH AMERICA

surfing

football

motor racing

football

Did you know?

Did you know?

• There are different types of football, such as American football, Australian football and Gaelic football.
• Blind people use a ball filled with ball bearings, so that they can hear it.
• Bright orange footballs are used when it is snowy.

• Hockey can be played on ice, on a field or under the water.
• A hockey stick can be shaped like a J or an L.
• Hockey was played in Egypt thousands of years ago.

polo

Look through the maps in this atlas to find the other sports and activities shown below.

▼

curling

baseball

skiing

yachting

Sports and Activities

e a n

chess

ASIA

Pacific

Ocean

karate

hockey

cricket

RICA

Indian

Ocean

Did you know?

ricket

- To surf you stand or lie on a board and float on the waves of the sea.
- Dolphins and whales like to surf the waves.
- The word surf can also mean to look at different pages of the World Wide Web on a computer.

Australian football

OCEANIA

tennis

surfing

rugby

sumo wrestling

lacrosse

scuba diving

gymnastics

World

Seas and oceans cover two thirds of the earth's surface. The rest is land. The land is divided up into seven large masses of land known as continents.

Greenland

Arctic

Mount McKinley

Rocky Mountains

NORTH AMERICA

R. Missouri

Niagara Falls

Yosemite Falls

R. Mississippi

EUROP

Atlas Mountains

Sahar Deser

The map shows some of the largest features on each continent.

Caribbean Sea

Atlantic Ocean

Pacific Ocean

Andes

Angel Falls

R. Amazon

SOUTH AMERICA

Andes

Did you know?

- The Sahara is the world's largest desert.
- The highest sand dunes are found in Algeria in Africa.
- The highest temperatures in the world occur in the Sahara, however the nights can be very cold.

Did you know?

- The world's highest mountain range is Himalaya.
- Mount Everest is the highest peak at 8848 metres (29 029 feet).
- Mount Everest was formed about 60 million years ago.

Nan Des

Iguazu Falls

Aconcagua

A global view of each continent is shown here. ▶

North America lies between the Atlantic and Pacific Oceans.

South America stretches from the Caribbean Sea towards the South Pole.

Europe is one of the smallest continents.

Natural Features

ean

Ural Mountains

R. Ob'

S i b e r i a

R. Volga

Caucasus

Black Sea

El'brus

Caspian Sea

A S I A

Kunlun Shan

Gobi Desert

Pacific

Ocean

rranean Sea

Himalaya

Chang Jiang

R. Nile

R. Ganges

Mount Everest

Arabian

Peninsula

Bay of Bengal

South China Sea

Arabian Sea

RICA

Indian Ocean

Borneo

R. Congo

Kilimanjaro

Puncak Jaya

New Guinea

Did you know?

ctoria Falls

- Angel Falls, in Venezuela, is the world's highest waterfall at 979 metres (3212 feet).

Great Sandy Desert

Kalahari Desert

- Victoria Falls, on the Zambezi river between Zambia and Zimbabwe, is the largest.

O C E A N I A

Great Victoria Desert

Tugela Falls

- Niagara Falls is the most powerful falls in North America.

frica is almost equally balanced either side of the Equator.

Asia is the largest continent.

Oceania is made up of Australia and many small islands.

Antarctica encircles the South Pole.

World

Continents are divided up into many different countries. There are over 190 countries in the world. Lines are drawn on the map to show where two countries meet. These are known as international boundaries.

GREENLAND
(Denmark)

U.S.A.

C A N A D A

More detailed maps of Europe can be found on pages 22-29

Paris
is the largest city in Western Europe

UNITED STATES
OF AMERICA

Azores
(Portugal)

TUNISIA

MOROCCO

ALGERIA   LIBY

WESTERN
SAHARA

THE
BAHAMAS

MEXICO

CUBA

DOMINICAN
REP.

HAITI

MAURITANIA

MALI   NIGER

Mexico City
is the largest city in North America

BELIZE

JAMAICA

PUERTO
RICO
(USA)

CAPE VERDE

SENEGAL

CH

GUATEMALA

HONDURAS

THE GAMBIA

BURKINA
FASO

EL SALVADOR   NICARAGUA

GUINEA-BISSAU

GUINEA

BENIN
TOGO

NIGERIA

COSTA RICA

TRINIDAD
& TOBAGO

CÔTE
D'IVOIRE

GHANA

Lagos
is the largest city in Africa

CEN
AFR
REP

PANAMA

VENEZUELA

SIERRA
LEONE

This map also shows the largest city in each continent.

GUYANA

SURINAME

FRENCH
GUIANA

LIBERIA

CAMEROON

EQUITORIAL
GUINEA

COLOMBIA

GABON

CONGO

Galapagos Is
(Ecuador)

ECUADOR

P
E
R
U

B R A Z I L

ANGO

FRENCH
POLYNESIA

Did you know?

When it is 12 noon in New York the time is
• 5 pm in London
• 3 am in Sydney
• 8 pm in Moscow
• Midnight in Bangkok

BOLIVIA

PARAGUAY

Sao Paulo
is the largest city in South America

NAM

C
H
I
L
E

A
R
G
E
N
T
I
N
A

URUGUAY

Did you know?

These countries have two capital cities.
• The Netherlands has The Hague and Amsterdam
• Malaysia has Kuala Lumpur and Putrajaya
• Bolivia has La Paz and Sucre

South Africa has three capitals - Pretoria, Cape Town and Bloemfontein

The flags of the eight largest countries in the world are shown below. Look through the rest of the atlas to find out more interesting facts about life in these countries.
▼

Falkland Islands
(UK)

South Georgia
(UK)

Russian Federation	Canada	China	United States of America
17 075 400 square kilometres 6 592 849 square miles	9 984 670 square kilometres 3 855 103 square miles	9 620 671 square kilometres 3 714 562 square miles	9 826 635 square kilometres 3 794 085 square miles

Countries and Cities

RUSSIAN FEDERATION

KAZAKHSTAN

MONGOLIA

stanbul
the largest
ty in Europe

GEORGIA

UZBEKISTAN

KYRGYZSTAN

N. KOREA

JAPAN

TURKEY

ARMENIA

AZERBAIJAN

TURKMENISTAN

TAJIKISTAN

S. KOREA

○ **Tokyo**
is the largest city
in Asia

CYPRUS

SYRIA

LEBANON

IRAQ

ISRAEL

JORDAN

KUWAIT

IRAN

**AFGHAN-
ISTAN**

PAKISTAN

CHINA

GYPT

SAUDI

BAHRAIN

QATAR

**UNITED ARAB
EMIRATES**

NEPAL

BHUTAN

ARABIA

OMAN

INDIA

**BANGLA-
DESH**

**MYANMAR
(BURMA)**

LAOS

VIETNAM

UDAN

ERITREA

YEMEN

THAILAND

CAMBODIA

PHILIPPINES

*Northern
Mariana Is.
(USA)*

**MARSHALL
ISLANDS**

**SOUTH
SUDAN**

ETHIOPIA

SOMALIA

**SRI
LANKA**

BRUNEI

MALAYSIA

PALAU

**FED. STATES OF
MICRONESIA**

UGANDA

MALDIVES

OCRATIC

KENYA

BLIC

RWANDA

HE

BURUNDI

O

SINGAPORE

INDONESIA

NAURU

KIRIBATI

TANZANIA

SEYCHELLES

**PAPUA
NEW
GUINEA**

**SOLOMON
ISLANDS**

TUVALU

MBIA

COMOROS

MALAWI

MOZAMBIQUE

MAURITIUS

MBABWE

MADAGASCAR

WANA

SWAZILAND

LESOTHO

**OF
TH
CA**

**EAST
TIMOR**

VANUATU

SAMOA

*New
Caledonia
(France)*

FIJI

TONGA

Did you know?

The time taken to fly between
- Los Angeles and Sydney is 14½ hours
- London and Tokyo is 12½ hours
- Paris and New York is 8½ hours

AUSTRALIA

○ **Sydney**
is the largest city
in Oceania

**NEW
ZEALAND**

*Îles Kerguélen
(France)*

Brazil	Australia	India	Argentina
8 514 879 square kilometres	7 692 024 square kilometres	3 064 989 square kilometres	2 766 889 square kilometres
3 287 613 square miles	2 969 907 square miles	1 183 364 square miles	1 068 302 square miles

North America

⑦ North America is the largest continent in the western hemisphere. It is surrounded by great oceans: the Arctic to the north, the Pacific to the west and the Atlantic to the east. The countries of North America are a mixture of the large nations of Canada, USA and Mexico in the north and the tiny Caribbean island nations in the south. It is joined to South America by the narrow strip of land known as the isthmus of Panama.

Facts

- Area: 24 680 331 square kilometres (9 529 129 square miles)
- Largest country: Canada 9 984 670 square kilometres (3 855 103 square miles)
- Longest river: Mississippi-Missouri 5969 kilometres (3709 miles)
- Highest mountain: Mount McKinley 6194 metres (20 321 feet)
- Largest lake: Lake Superior 82 100 square kilometres (31 698 square miles)
- Largest island: Greenland 2 175 600 square kilometres (840 004 square miles)

Try this!

Unscramble these letters to find an island name.
Clue: It is the largest island in North America.

G L D E A N R E N

Answers at the back of the atlas.

N
W   E
S

GREENLAND
(Denmark)

□ Nuuk

Baffin Bay

Baffin Island

Hudson Bay

CANADA

Arctic Ocean

Rocky

ALASKA
U.S.A.

▲ Mount McKinley

○ **Anchorage**

Bering Sea

⑥

⑤

Where in the world is North America?

Atlantic Ocean

Pacific Ocean

Gulf of Mexico

Caribbean Sea

SOUTH AMERICA

Did you know?
• 2 million caribou live in Canada.

Cities and countries

Seattle
San Francisco
Los Angeles
Phoenix
Denver
Minneapolis
Chicago
St Louis
Detroit
Toronto
Ottawa
Montreal
Boston
New York
Washington D.C.
Atlanta
Dallas
Houston
New Orleans
Miami

Lake Superior
R. Missouri
R. Mississippi
ountains

UNITED STATES OF AMERICA

Monterrey
Guadalajara
Mexico City
Puebla
MEXICO

Belmopan
BELIZE
GUATEMALA
Guatemala City
San Salvador
EL SALVADOR
Tegucigalpa
HONDURAS
Managua
NICARAGUA
San José
COSTA RICA
Panama City
PANAMA

Havana
CUBA
Nassau
THE BAHAMAS
Kingston
JAMAICA
HAITI
Port-au-Prince
Santo Domingo
DOMINICAN REPUBLIC
San Juan
PUERTO RICO (USA)

Bermuda (UK)

ST KITTS AND NEVIS
ANTIGUA AND BARBUDA
DOMINICA
BARBADOS
ST LUCIA
ST VINCENT AND THE GRENADINES
GRENADA

A   B   C   D
1
2
3

3

Canada

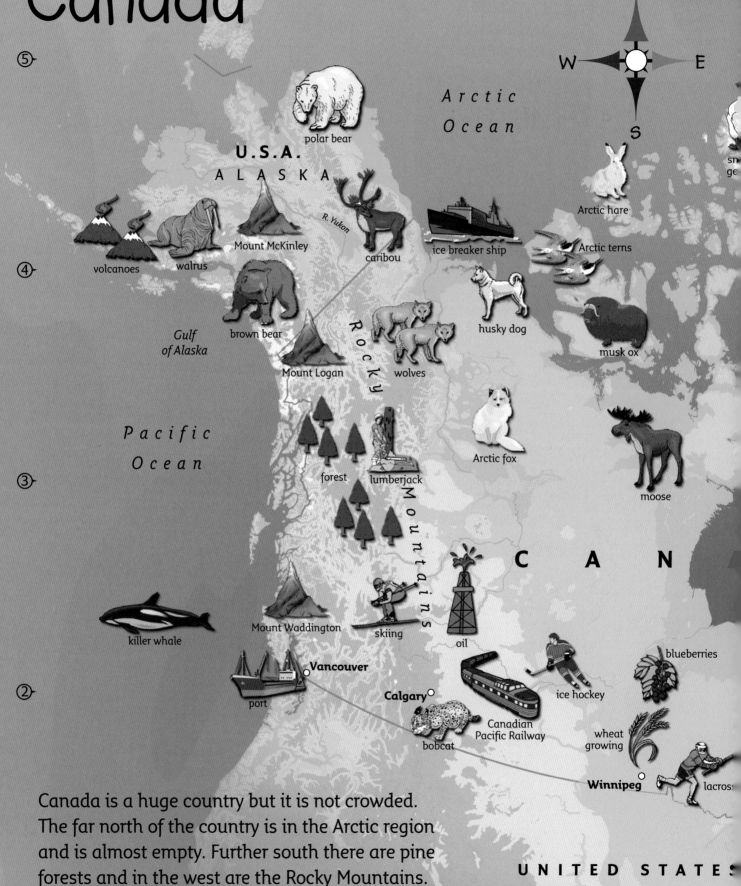

⑤

N

W ← → E

S

Arctic Ocean

polar bear

U.S.A.
A L A S K A

R. Yukon

Arctic hare

④

volcanoes

walrus

Mount McKinley

caribou

ice breaker ship

Arctic terns

musk ox

Gulf of Alaska

brown bear

Mount Logan

wolves

husky dog

Pacific Ocean

forest

lumberjack

Arctic fox

moose

③

R o c k y   M o u n t a i n s

C   **A**   **N**

killer whale

Mount Waddington

skiing

oil

Vancouver

blueberries

②

port

Calgary

Canadian Pacific Railway

ice hockey

bobcat

wheat growing

Winnipeg

lacross

Canada is a huge country but it is not crowded.
The far north of the country is in the Arctic region
and is almost empty. Further south there are pine
forests and in the west are the Rocky Mountains.

U N I T E D   S T A T E S
O F   A M E R I C A

①

Ⓐ   Ⓑ   Ⓒ

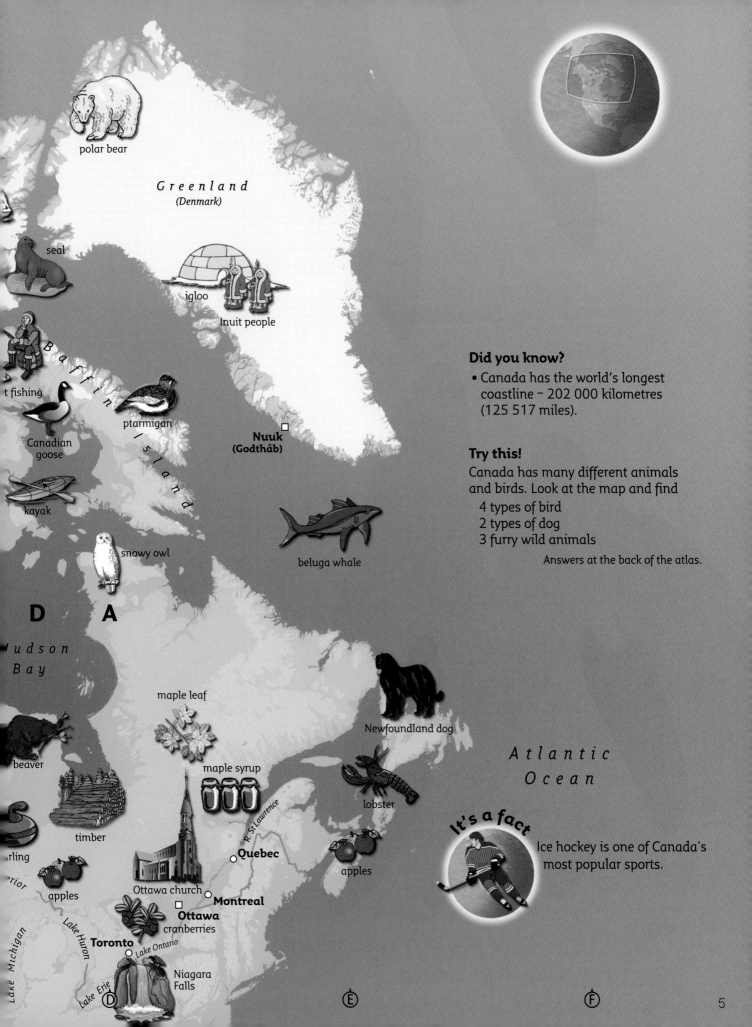

polar bear

Greenland
(Denmark)

seal

igloo

Inuit people

t fishing

B a f f i n   I s l a n d

ptarmigan

Canadian goose

kayak

snowy owl

Nuuk
(Godthåb)

beluga whale

D   **A**

*H u d s o n
B a y*

maple leaf

Newfoundland dog

beaver

*A t l a n t i c
O c e a n*

maple syrup

timber

lobster

R. St Lawrence

Quebec

apples

It's a fact

Ice hockey is one of Canada's most popular sports.

rling

erior

apples

Ottawa church

Montreal

Ottawa
cranberries

Toronto

Lake Ontario

Lake Michigan

Lake Huron

Lake Erie

Niagara Falls

Ⓓ   Ⓔ   Ⓕ

Did you know?

• Canada has the world's longest coastline – 202 000 kilometres (125 517 miles).

Try this!

Canada has many different animals and birds. Look at the map and find

4 types of bird
2 types of dog
3 furry wild animals

Answers at the back of the atlas.

United States of America

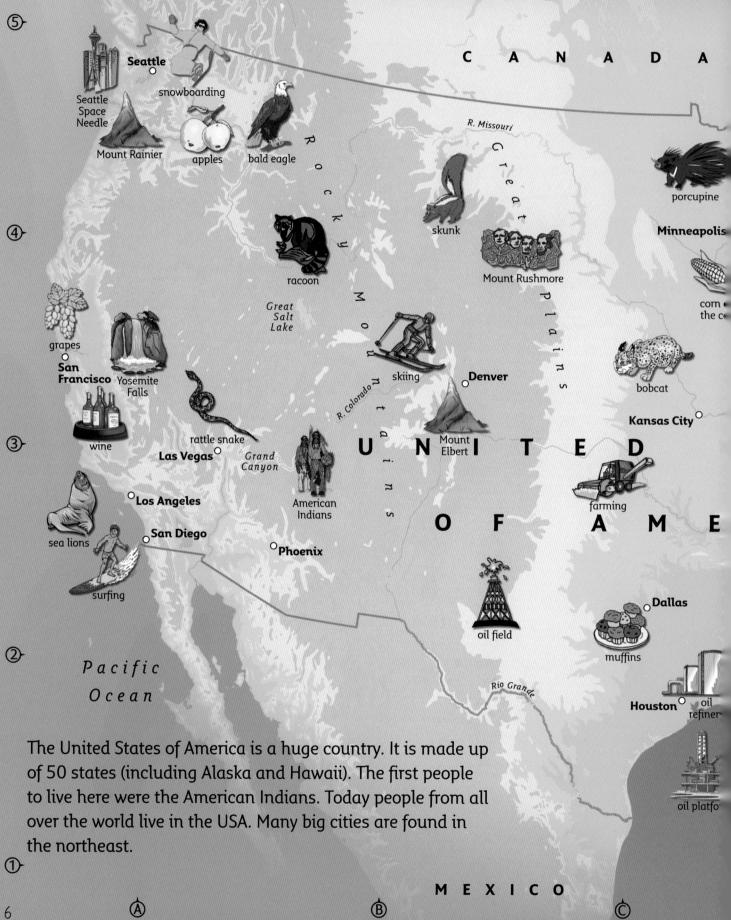

⑤

Seattle

snowboarding

Seattle Space Needle

Mount Rainier

apples

bald eagle

C A N A D A

R. Missouri

Rocky

Great

porcupine

④

skunk

Mount Rushmore

Minneapolis

racoon

corn the ce

Great Salt Lake

Mountains

grapes

San Francisco

Yosemite Falls

skiing

Denver

bobcat

wine

rattle snake

Mount Elbert

U N I T E D

Kansas City

③

Las Vegas

Grand Canyon

R. Colorado

American Indians

farming

Los Angeles

O F   A M E

sea lions

San Diego

Phoenix

oil field

Dallas

surfing

muffins

②

Pacific Ocean

Rio Grande

Houston

oil refiner

The United States of America is a huge country. It is made up of 50 states (including Alaska and Hawaii). The first people to live here were the American Indians. Today people from all over the world live in the USA. Many big cities are found in the northeast.

oil platfo

①

M E X I C O

Ⓐ   Ⓑ   Ⓒ

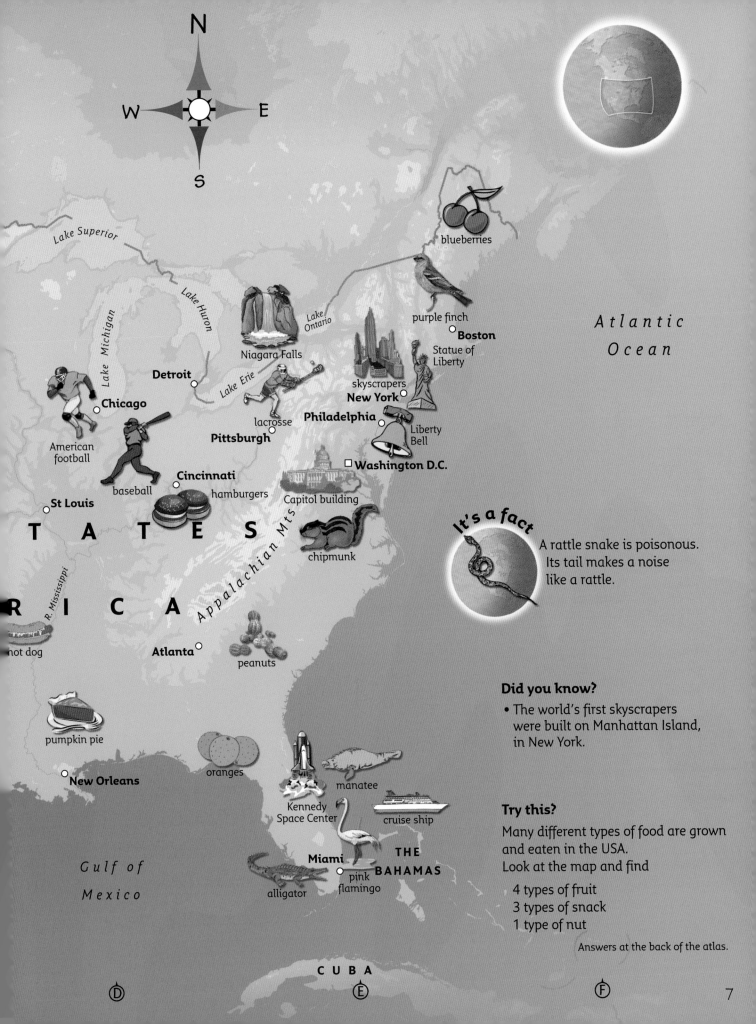

N
W E
S

Lake Superior

Lake Michigan
Lake Huron
Lake Ontario
Lake Erie

blueberries

purple finch

Boston

Statue of Liberty

Niagara Falls

skyscrapers

New York

Detroit

lacrosse

Philadelphia

Liberty Bell

Chicago

American football

Pittsburgh

baseball

Cincinnati

hamburgers

☐ **Washington D.C.**

Capitol building

St Louis

T A T E S

Appalachian Mts.

chipmunk

R I C A

R. Mississippi

hot dog

Atlanta

peanuts

Atlantic Ocean

It's a fact

A rattle snake is poisonous. Its tail makes a noise like a rattle.

Did you know?

• The world's first skyscrapers were built on Manhattan Island, in New York.

pumpkin pie

New Orleans

oranges

Kennedy Space Center

manatee

cruise ship

Gulf of Mexico

alligator

Miami

pink flamingo

THE BAHAMAS

Try this?

Many different types of food are grown and eaten in the USA.
Look at the map and find

4 types of fruit
3 types of snack
1 type of nut

Answers at the back of the atlas.

C U B A

Ⓓ   Ⓔ   Ⓕ   7

Mexico and the Caribbean

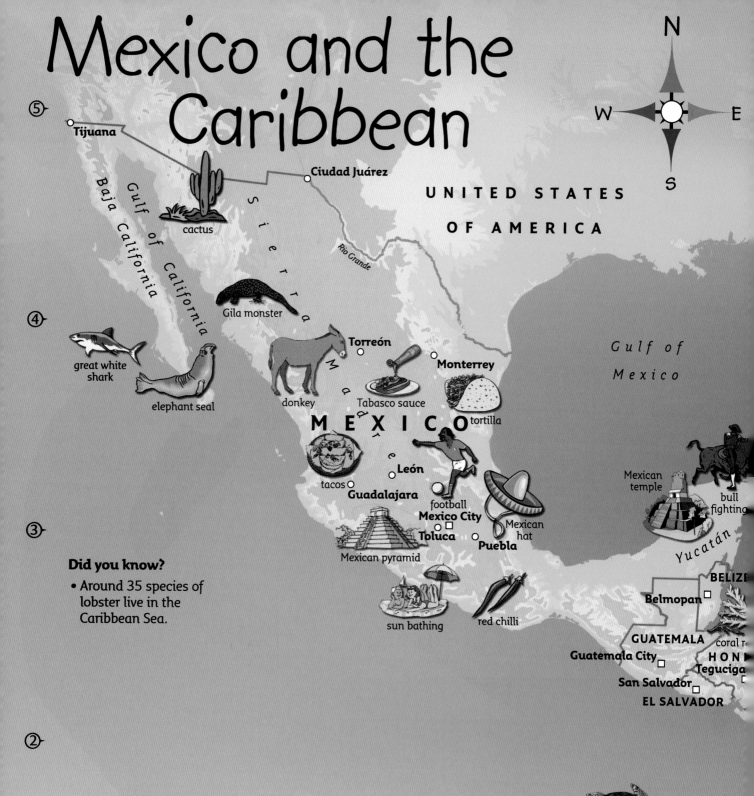

⑤

⑤ Tijuana

Baja California

Gulf of California

Sierra Madre

Ciudad Juárez

Rio Grande

UNITED STATES

OF AMERICA

N
W E
S

cactus

④ great white shark

elephant seal

Gila monster

donkey

Torreón

Tabasco sauce

Monterrey

tortilla

Gulf of Mexico

M E X I C O

③ **Did you know?**
• Around 35 species of lobster live in the Caribbean Sea.

tacos

Guadalajara

León

football

Mexico City

Toluca

Mexican pyramid

Puebla

Mexican hat

Mexican temple

bull fighting

Yucatán

BELIZE

Belmopan

②

sun bathing

red chilli

GUATEMALA

Guatemala City

coral r

H O N

Teguciga

San Salvador

EL SALVADOR

turtle

It's a fact
Sea horses can move their eyes all around, without moving their bodies.

Pacific

Ocean

①

8   Ⓐ   Ⓑ   Ⓒ

The land between the USA and South America is known as Central America. Mexico is the largest country here. There is dry desert in northern Mexico and wet rainforest in southern Central America. The Caribbean is the area to the east, where there are hundreds of tropical islands.

Bermuda

Atlantic Ocean

Try this!
Many different species of fish and birds are found in this region.
Look at the map and find

6 types of fish and sea animals
2 types of bird

Answers at the back of the atlas.

cruise ship

☐ Nassau

THE BAHAMAS

Havana ☐

C U B A   Monarch butterfly

cigars

sugar cane

mangoes   reggae singer

Cayman Is

Turks and Caicos Islands

limes

DOMINICAN REPUBLIC

HAITI   Santo Domingo

Port-au-Prince ☐

parrot

San Juan ☐

cruise ship   **ST KITTS AND NEVIS**

Anguilla

ANTIGUA AND BARBUDA

Montserrat
Guadeloupe

scuba diving

butterflies

JAMAICA   ☐ **Kingston**

rum

Caribbean

gourds

Sea

bananas

radio telescope

PUERTO RICO

volcano   **DOMINICA**

Martinique

pineapples

sea horse

ST LUCIA

ST VINCENT AND THE GRENADINES   **BARBADOS**

GRENADA

S

bananas

CARAGUA

toucan

tropical fish

monk seal

Aruba

oil platform

yachting   **TRINIDAD & TOBAGO**

cricket

anagua

Lake Nicaragua

OSTA RICA

☐ **San José**

Panama Canal

coconuts

Panama City ☐

P A N A M A

coffee

monkey

V E N E Z U E L A

C O L O M B I A

South America

⑦ South America stretches farther south from the equator than all the other continents. The longest mountain range in the world, the Andes, runs the full length of the continent. The Amazon rainforest is the largest in the world. Colourful birds and butterflies, giant snakes, jaguars, monkeys and pumas can all be found in this lush forest. People speak Portuguese in Brazil, but Spanish in other countries.

10

⑥

⑤

Atlantic Ocean

Pacific Ocean

TRINIDAD & TOBAGO
Port of Spain

Caracas
VENEZUELA

Georgetown
Paramaribo
Cayenne

GUYANA
SURINAME
FRENCH GUIANA

Bogotá
COLOMBIA

Quito
ECUADOR

Amazon Basin
R. Amazon

BRAZIL

Lima
PERU

Lake Titicaca

La Paz
BOLIVIA
Sucre

Brasília

Belo Horizonte

Galapagos Islands
(Ecuador)

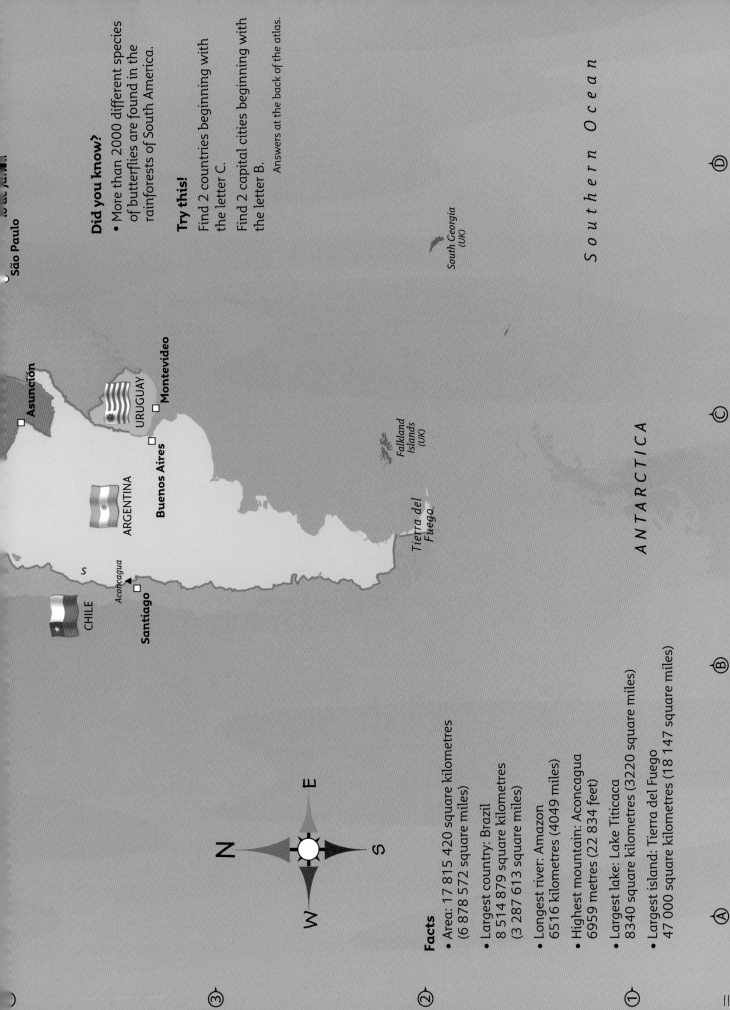

São Paulo

Did you know?

- More than 2000 different species of butterflies are found in the rainforests of South America.

Try this!

Find 2 countries beginning with the letter C.

Find 2 capital cities beginning with the letter B.

Answers at the back of the atlas.

Asunción

URUGUAY

Montevideo

ARGENTINA

Buenos Aires

South Georgia
(UK)

Falkland
Islands
(UK)

Tierra del
Fuego

Aconcagua

CHILE

Santiago

Southern Ocean

ANTARCTICA

N
E
S
W

Facts

- Area: 17 815 420 square kilometres
  (6 878 572 square miles)

- Largest country: Brazil
  8 514 879 square kilometres
  (3 287 613 square miles)

- Longest river: Amazon
  6516 kilometres (4049 miles)

- Highest mountain: Aconcagua
  6959 metres (22 834 feet)

- Largest lake: Lake Titicaca
  8340 square kilometres (3220 square miles)

- Largest island: Tierra del Fuego
  47 000 square kilometres (18 147 square miles)

Ⓐ Ⓑ Ⓒ Ⓓ

① ② ③

11

South America North

⑤

Most people in this area live on the low land near the coast.
Ecuador is the Spanish word for equator. The equator is an
imaginary line around the middle of the earth. Many unique
species of animal live in the area. Potatoes, peppers and
beans have been grown here for thousands of years.

Caribbean Sea

④

Barranquilla
Cartagena

Maracaibo

Barquisimeto

Caracas

Valencia

Port of Spain

TRINIDAD & TOBAGO

oil refineries

oil wells

R. Orinoco

PANAMA

Bucaramanga

iguana

puma

jaguar

VENEZUELA

GUYA

Angel Falls

poison arrow frog

Medellín

Bogotá

coffee

emeralds

Guiana

③

Cali

COLOMBIA

H

slot

Quito

Mount Cotopaxi

ECUADOR

coffee

R. Negro

butterflies

Mana

manta ray

Guayaquil

football

capybara

tapir

Amazon Basin

condor

②

panpipes

monkeys

R. Madeira

anaconda

B

Pacific Ocean

llama

Andes

rubber

deforestation

①

Lima

PERU

coffee

BOLIVIA

12

Ⓐ

Ⓑ

Ⓒ

N
W ● E
S

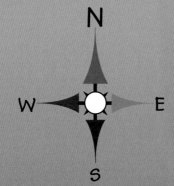

Andean panpipes are musical instruments made from pipes strapped together.

Georgetown

Paramaribo
rocket
launch

Cayenne

SURINAME

FRENCH GUIANA

Atlantic Ocean

cayenne peppers

hlands

Did you know?

• The Amazon is the largest rainforest in the world. About half of the world's plants, animals and insects are found there.

Try this!

Look at the map and find

2 precious stones
1 deadly snake

Answers at the back of the atlas.

R. Amazon

Belém

Fortaleza

toucan

armadillo

sugar cane

Natal

surfing

R **A** **Z** **I** **L**

Recife

R. São Francisco

R. Tocantins

Maceió

porcupines

parrot

B r a z i l i a n

H i g h l a n d s

D diamonds

E

F

lobster

Salvador

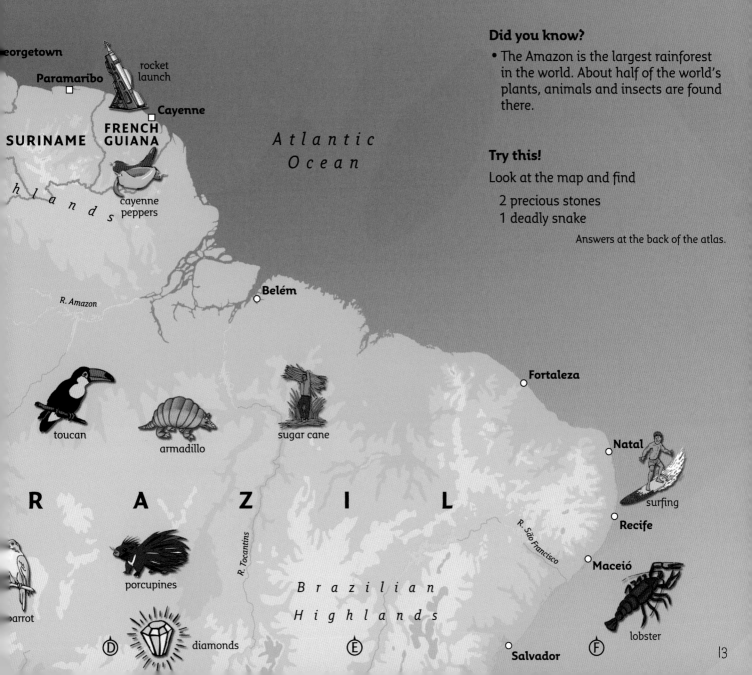

13

South America South

Running down the west coast of this area is the driest place on earth, the Atacama Desert. The southern tip of South America is very cold and there are icebergs in the sea. Many people in Paraguay are descended from the Indians who lived in South America before people from Europe arrived.

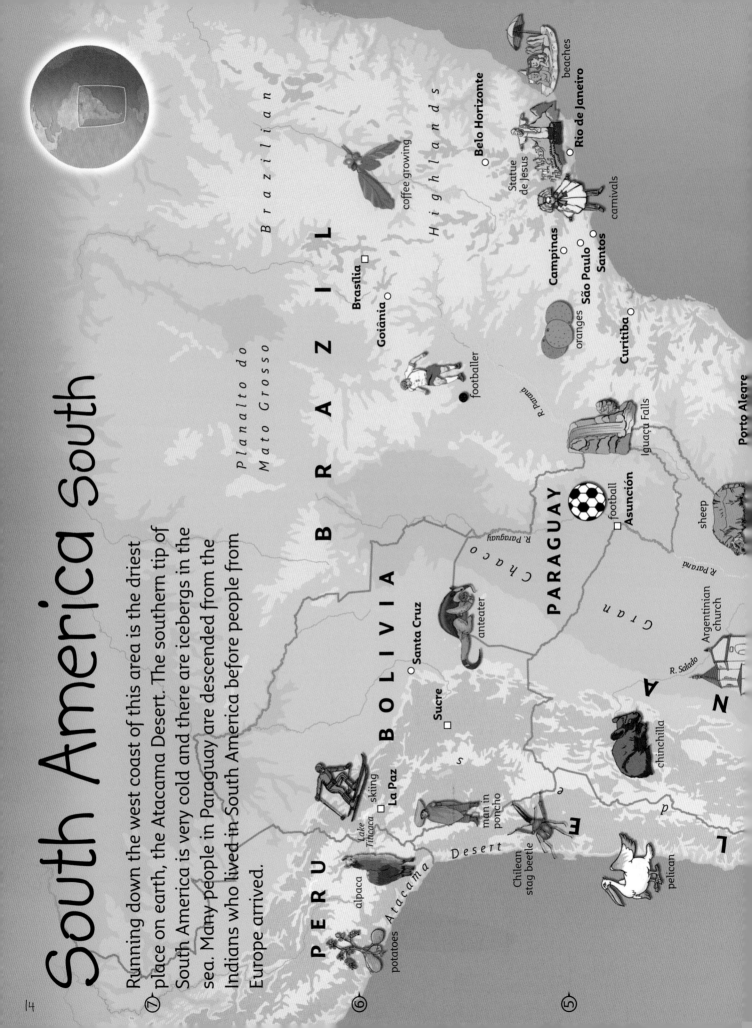

Brazilian

Highlands

coffee growing

beaches

Belo Horizonte

Statue de Jesus

Rio de Janeiro

carnivals

Campinas

São Paulo

Santos

oranges

Curitiba

footballer

B R A Z I L

Brasília

Goiânia

Planalto do Mato Grosso

R. Paraná

Iguaçu Falls

Porto Alegre

R. Paraná

PARAGUAY

football

Asunción

R. Paraguay

Chaco

Gran

sheep

Argentinian church

R. Salado

B O L I V I A

Santa Cruz

anteater

Sucre

chinchilla

s

e

p

L

P E R U

alpaca

potatoes

Lake Titicaca

skiing

La Paz

man in poncho

Atacama   Desert

Chilean stag beetle

pelican

N

E

N **E** **S** **W**

Did you know?
• Chile is 10 times longer than it is wide.

Try this!
Look at the map and find
2 types of fish
Many sports are played in South America
Can you name 3 of these?

Answers at the back of the atlas.

It's a fact
Anteaters have a long, sticky tongue and no teeth.

mackerel

South Georgia (UK)

oil tanker

sardines

Atlantic Ocean

URUGUAY

Montevideo

Río de la Plata

polo

Rosario

Buenos Aires

motor racing

tango dancers

wine

Córdoba

gaucho

R. Negro

Mendoza

vineyards

Aconcagua

Santiago

wine

grapes

Chilean chapel

Pacific Ocean

fishing boats

puma

glaciers

penguins

elephant seals

Tierra del Fuego

Cape Horn

albatross

Falkland Islands (UK)

southern whale

killer whale

Ⓐ Ⓑ Ⓒ Ⓓ

① ② ③

15

Africa

Africa is the second largest continent. It is 3 times the area of Europe. From the Mediterranean Sea in the north, Africa stretches approximately 8000 kilometres (4971 miles) to its most southerly point, Cape Agulhas. Most of northern Africa lies in and around the Sahara desert, while large areas of central Africa are covered in dense tropical rainforest.

Facts

- Area: 30 343 578 square kilometres (11 715 721 square miles)
- Largest country: Algeria 2 381 741 square kilometres (919 595 square miles)
- Longest river: Nile 6695 kilometres (4160 miles)
- Highest mountain: Kilimanjaro 5892 metres (19 331 feet)
- Largest lake: Lake Victoria 68 800 square kilometres (26 563 square miles)
- Largest island: Madagascar 587 040 square kilometres (226 657 square miles)

EUROPE

ASIA

A S I A

Red Sea

Mediterranean Sea

S a h a r a

Atlas Mountains

Azores
(Portugal)

Madeira
(Portugal)

Canary Is
(Spain)

Rabat
MOROCCO

Laayoune
WESTERN SAHARA

Nouakchott
MAURITANIA

Dakar
SENEGAL
Banjul
THE GAMBIA
Bissau
GUINEA-BISSAU
Conakry
GUINEA
Freetown
Monrovia

Praia
CAPE VERDE

Algiers
ALGERIA

Tunis
TUNISIA

Tripoli
LIBYA

Cairo
EGYPT

R. Nile

Khartoum
SUDAN

Asmara
ERITREA

Djibouti
DJIBOUTI

Ethiopian Highlands

Addis Ababa
ETHIOPIA

Juba
SOUTH SUDAN

SOMALIA

Ndjamena
CHAD

CENTRAL AFRICAN REPUBLIC

Bangui

Niamey
NIGER

Abuja
NIGERIA
Porto-Novo

Bamako
MALI

Ouagadougou
BURKINA FASO

Yamoussoukro
CÔTE D'IVOIRE

GHANA
Lomé
BENIN
Accra

CAMEROON

⑦

⑥

⑤

16

SEYCHELLES
Victoria

MAURITIUS
Port Louis

Reunion (France)

Indian Ocean

COMOROS
Moroni

Mayotte (France)

Antananarivo

MADAGASCAR

KENYA
Nairobi
▲ *Kilimanjaro*

Lake Victoria

RWANDA
Kigali

Bujumbura

BURUNDI

Dodoma

TANZANIA

MALAWI
Lilongwe

Lusaka

Harare

MOZAMBIQUE

ZIMBABWE

SWAZILAND

Maputo

Pretoria (Tshwane)

Mbabane

Maseru

LESOTHO

DEMOCRATIC REPUBLIC OF THE CONGO

Kinshasa

ZAMBIA

BOTSWANA
Gaborone

Bloemfontein

REPUBLIC OF SOUTH AFRICA

Cape Agulhas

CONGO

Brazzaville

GABON

Luanda

ANGOLA

NAMIBIA

Windhoek

Cape Town

TOGO

SÃO TOMÉ & PRÍNCIPE

EQUATORIAL GUINEA

Ascension Island (UK)

St Helena (UK)

Atlantic Ocean

③

Where in the World is Africa?

②

Did you know?

- The Goliath beetle found near the equator in Africa is one of the largest insects in the world.

①

Ⓐ Ⓑ Ⓒ Ⓓ

N
W E
S

Try this!

Unscramble these letters to find the country.
Clue: It is surrounded by sea.

C A R D A M S A G A

Answers at the back of the atlas.

Northern Africa

⑤

Did you know?
• In Nigeria, twins are always called the same names. The first twin is called Taiwo. The second twin is called Kehinde.

④

③

②

①

N
W **E**
S

SPAIN

PORTUGAL

Mediter

Madeira
(Portugal)

Algiers

spices

citrus fruit

grapes

Rabat
Casablanca

MOROCCO

Atlas Mts

Berber architecture

oasis

Canary Is
(Spain)

A L G E R I A

S

a

sand dur

Laayoune

WESTERN SAHARA

date palm

cactus

camel

dates

MAURITANIA

baboon

M A L I

CAPE VERDE

Nouakchott

R. Sénégal

Praia

S

a

h

e

l

N I

R. Niger

Dakar

SENEGAL

Banjul

THE GAMBIA

groundnuts

Niamey

beach resort

Bissau

GUINEA-BISSAU

pygmy hippopotamus

GUINEA

Bamako

hoopoe

BURKINA FASO

Ouagadougou

N I G E

Conakry

BENIN

Freetown

GHANA

TOGO

Abuj

SIERRA LEONE

bananas

CÔTE D'IVOIRE

cocoa

Lake Volta

football

Monrovia

Yamoussoukro

Lomé

Lagos

LIBERIA

Accra

Porto-Novo

Mt Camer

Malabo

coconuts

Gulf of Guinea

oil

São Tomé

EQUAT GUINE

Librev

SÃO TOMÉ AND PRÍNCIPE

A t l a n t i c

O c e a n

Africa is connected to the continent of Asia at the narrow Sinai peninsula, north of the Red Sea. It is separated narrowly from Europe by the Strait of Gibraltar. Much of northern Africa is dry desert: the Sahara Desert and the Sahel region.

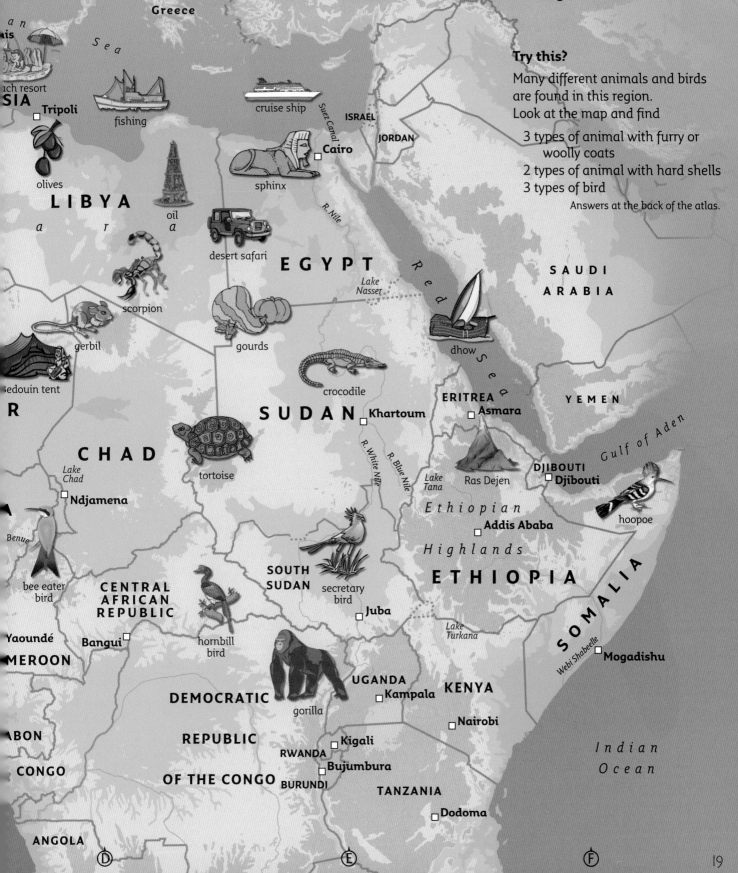

ITALY

Greece

an
Sea

ITALY
ch resort
SIA

Tripoli

fishing

cruise ship

Suez Canal

ISRAEL

JORDAN

Cairo

sphinx

R. Nile

olives

LIBYA

oil

a
r
a

desert safari

EGYPT

Lake
Nasser

scorpion

Red Sea

dhow

SAUDI
ARABIA

gourds

gerbil

Bedouin tent

R

crocodile

ERITREA

YEMEN

Asmara

Gulf of Aden

CHAD

SUDAN

Khartoum

Lake
Chad

Ndjamena

tortoise

R. White Nile

R. Blue Nile

Lake
Tana

Ras Dejen

DJIBOUTI

Djibouti

hoopoe

Ethiopian

Benue

Addis Ababa

Highlands

bee eater
bird

CENTRAL
AFRICAN
REPUBLIC

SOUTH
SUDAN

secretary
bird

ETHIOPIA

Yaoundé

Bangui

hornbill
bird

Juba

Lake
Turkana

MEROON

gorilla

UGANDA

Kampala

KENYA

SOMALIA

Webi Shabeelle

Mogadishu

DEMOCRATIC

Nairobi

ABON

REPUBLIC

Kigali

Indian
Ocean

CONGO

OF THE CONGO

RWANDA

BURUNDI

Bujumbura

TANZANIA

ANGOLA

Dodoma

D

E

F

Try this?

Many different animals and birds are found in this region.
Look at the map and find

3 types of animal with furry or woolly coats
2 types of animal with hard shells
3 types of bird

Answers at the back of the atlas.

Southern Africa

⑦ At the centre of southern Africa is the huge rainforest of the River Congo and the Congo Basin. The Great Rift Valley is surrounded by some of the highest mountains in Africa. In the southwest are the Kalahari and Namib deserts.

N
W E
S

DJIBOUTI

ERITREA

SOMALIA

Mogadishu

Indian Ocean

ETHIOPIA

Ethiopian Highlands

coffee beans

cloves

beaches

Dar es Salaam

lion

Moroni

COMOROS

MAYOTTE

KENYA

Lake Turkana

elephants

Kilimanjaro

Dodoma

chameleon

Lake Nyasa

SUDAN

secretary bird

Juba

UGANDA

Kampala

Nairobi

Lake Victoria

leopard

TANZANIA

MALA...

SOUTH SUDAN

gorilla

RWANDA Kigali

Bujumbura

BURUNDI

Great Rift Valley

Lake Tanganyika

CENTRAL AFRICAN REPUBLIC

Bangui

hornbill bird

R. Congo

DEMOCRATIC REPUBLIC OF THE CONGO

Lubumbashi

cheetah

crocodiles

Congo Basin

elephants

NIGERIA

CAMEROON

Yaoundé

chimpanzee

deforestation

Kinshasa

C O N G O

Brazzaville

ANGOLA

ANGOLA

Bie Plateau

GABON

Libreville

EQUATORIAL GUINEA

Malabo

São Tomé

SÃO TOMÉ AND PRÍNCIPE

flying fish

Luanda

oil rig

⑥

⑤

MADAGASCAR

Antananarivo

crocodiles

lemur

Mozambique Channel

aardvark

MOZAMBIQUE

port

Harare

ZIMBABWE

Lusaka

rhinoceros

R. Limpopo

Victoria Falls

Maputo

Mbabane

SWAZILAND

Zulu warrior

Zulu house

Durban

Pretoria (Tshwane)

Johannesburg

Gaborone

BOTSWANA

meerkat

Kalahari Desert

oryx

Bloemfontein

Maseru

LESOTHO

Drakensberg

R. Orange

REPUBLIC OF SOUTH AFRICA

Port Elizabeth

cricket

NAMIBIA

Windhoek

rhinoceros

rugby

sand dunes

Namib Desert

ostrich

oranges

grapes

Cape Town

Cape of Good Hope

penguins

Atlantic Ocean

sardines

sharks

Did you know?

- Diamonds and gold are mined in southern Africa.

Try this?

There are lots of different fruits and plants in this region. Look at the map and find

2 types of fruit
1 type of spice.

Answers at the back of the atlas.

It's a fact

Gorillas are the largest type of ape in the world.

A   B   C   D

1   2   3

21

Europe

The land area of Europe covers just over 2% of the world. It is the second smallest continent and extends far north into the Arctic Ocean and south to the Mediterranean Sea. In the north the winters are long and cold. In the south the weather is much warmer. Europe has over 40 countries and a wide variety of cultures, languages and religions.

Where in the world is Europe?

ICELAND
Reykjavík

N
W   E
S

Faroe Islands
(Denmark)

UNITED KINGDOM

Dublin

Great Britain

IRELAND

London

NETHERLAN
Amsterd
The Hague

Bruss

BELGIUM

Paris

LUXEMBOU
B.

FRANCE

SWITZERL

ANDORRA

MONACC

PORTUGAL

Madrid

Barcelona

Lisbon

SPAIN

Gibraltar (UK)

Atlantic
Ocean

Try this!

How many flags are black, red and yellow?

Which flag has 5 blue stripes?

Which country uses this flag?

Answers at the back of the atlas.

A F R I C

⑤
④
③
②
①

Ⓐ   Ⓑ   Ⓒ

Facts

- Area: 9 908 599 square kilometres (3 825 731 square miles)
- Largest country: Ukraine 603 700 square kilometres (233 090 square miles) (excluding Russian Federation)
- Longest river: Volga 3688 kilometres (2291 miles)
- Highest mountain: El'brus 5642 metres (18 510 feet)
- Largest lake: Caspian Sea 371 000 square kilometres (143 243 square miles)
- Largest island: Great Britain 218 476 square kilometres (84 354 square miles)

Did you know?

- Vatican City is the smallest country in the world. It is the headquarters of the Roman Catholic Church.

United Kingdom and Ireland

⑦ The United Kingdom is made up of 4 nations: England, Wales, Scotland and Northern Ireland. Its capital and largest city is London. Great Britain is the largest island in Europe and is separated from mainland Europe by only 35 kilometres (21 miles) at the Strait of Dover. Ireland, whose capital is Dublin, is a separate country from Northern Ireland.

⑥

Try this!

Many different sports are popular in the United Kingdom. Look at the map and find

3 sports played with a ball
1 sport that takes place on water
2 sports that need ice or snow

Answers at the back of the atlas.

⑤

N

W — E

S

Shetland Islands

Orkney Islands

Atlantic Ocean

The Minch

Lewis

Skye

golden eagle

Inner Hebrides

Outer Hebrides

Highland cattle

Moray Firth

Inverness ○

Loch Ness

skiing

Ben Nevis

Fort William ○

Grampian Mts

S C O T L A N D

Highland piper

Jura

curling

Islay

Glasgow ○

Edinburgh ○

Firth of Forth

Edinburgh Castle

Dundee ○

Aberdeen ○

oil rig

fishing boat

Did you know?
• More than 300 different languages are spoken in London.

North

FRANCE

English Channel

Sea

North Channel

UNITED KINGDOM

NORTHERN IRELAND

Londonderry

Lough Neagh

Belfast

Dundalk Bay

Dundalk

harp

Dublin
Dublin courthouse

port

R. Shannon

dairy farming

Donegal Bay

potatoes

IRELAND

shamrock

Galway
Galway Bay

Limerick

Waterford

crystal glass

Cork

Irish dancers

Guinness

St George's Channel

Celtic Sea

yachting

Isle of Man

Manx cat

Irish Sea

Anglesey

Cardigan Bay

WALES

Cambrian Mountains

daffodil

Swansea

Cardiff
Bristol Channel

Land's End

Isles of Scilly

Plymouth

windsurfing

Torquay

Bournemouth

Newcastle upon Tyne

R. Tyne

Middlesbrough

R. Tees

cathedral

fishing boat

The Pennines

York

Leeds

Bradford

Manchester

rose

Blackpool

Preston

Liverpool

cricket

sheep

Sheffield

Stoke-on-Trent

Derby

Nottingham

R. Trent

Leicester

R. Severn

Wolverhampton

Birmingham

rugby

Bristol

Stonehenge

ENGLAND

football

Oxford

Reading

Southampton

Portsmouth

Isle of Wight

The Wash

Norwich

Norfolk Broads

Ipswich

port

Big Ben

London

R. Thames

London bus

Tower Bridge

Cambridge

Southend-on-Sea

Brighton

yachting

It's a fact

Red buses have been used in London since the 1950s.

Ⓐ Ⓑ Ⓒ Ⓓ

① ② ③

25

Northern Europe

⑤

□ **Reykjavík**

glaciers

ICELAND

Northern Europe has a rugged landscape and many of its countries are almost completely surrounded by sea. In the far north winters can be extremely cold and the seas may freeze for several months. Most people live in the south of this region where the climate is milder.

④

Faroe Is (Denmark)

fishing boats

salmon

Atlantic Ocean

③

Highland piper

oil rigs

Norwegi church

Edinburgh Castle

DE

North Sea

pigs

shamrock

IRELAND □ **Dublin**

UNITED

sheep

harp

windmills

KINGDOM

NETHERLANDS

Did you know?

• Parts of the Baltic Sea can be frozen for 6 months of the year.

②

Tower Bridge

Amsterdam □
The Hague

Gouda cheese

GE

rugby

London

Brussels □
BELGIUM

Frankfu

English Channel

LUXEMBOURG

Luxembourg

Try this!

Many different types of food are grown or manufactured in this region. Look at the map and find

Mont St Michel

Paris □

R. Loire

R. Seine

owl

Arc de Triomphe

Eiffel Tower

1 type of cheese
3 types of farm animal
① 1 type of pastry

seafood

Bern □

Answers at the back of the atlas.

Bay of Biscay

F R A N C E

SWITZERLAN

croissants

Massif Central

IT

Arctic Ocean

blue whale

puffin

owl

lemming

reindeer

moose

skiing

Oslo

Vänern

Vättern

badger

Copenhagen

RK

wind farms

R. Elbe

Berlin

ANY

football

Munich

castle

S

AUSTRIA

Lappland

wild mushrooms

FINLAND

Gulf of Bothnia

saunas

Helsinki

Stockholm

Tallinn

ESTONIA

LATVIA

Riga

LITHUANIA

Vilnius

RUS. FED.

Baltic Sea

North European

R. Vistula

Warsaw

POLAND

glass making

CZECH REPUBLIC

SLOVAKIA

Bratislava

Vienna

R. Danube

Budapest

HUNGARY

Plain

R. Dvina

Minsk

BELARUS

boar

brown bears

Carpathian Mts

Chisinau

MOLDOVA

castle

ROMANIA

eider duck

Kola Peninsula

fishing through ice

White Sea

wheat farming

R. Northern Dvina

paper making

Lake Onega

lynx

RUSSIAN

Lake Ladoga

St Petersburg

Winter Palace

R. Sukhona

beavers

wild horses

FEDERATION

dairy cows

Moscow

Kremlin

Volga Uplands

R. Dnieper

potatoes

Central Russian

Russian dolls

Uplands

It's a fact

Glass is made from sand. The sand is heated to a high temperature until it melts.

UKRAINE

R. Dniester

D   E   F   27

Southern Europe

DENMARK

North Sea

Hamburg

⑤

Atlantic

Ocean

UNITED KINGDOM

London

English Channel

NETHERLANDS
Amsterdam
The Hague

Brussels

BELGIUM

LUXEMBOURG

R. Rhine

Hannover

Berlin

GERMANY

Cologne

Frankfurt

Munich

Swiss cheese

grapes

Bern
LIECHTENSTEIN

SWITZERLAND

cast

football

AU S

R. Seine

Paris

apples

R. Loire

Arc de Triomphe

Eiffel Tower

FRANCE

croissants

cheese

Massif Central

skiing

④

seafood

Bay of Biscay

wine

garlic

Mont Blanc

cathedral

Milan

R. Po

gondola

R. Rhône

swordfish

Cantabrian Mts

Oporto

bull fighting

Spanish guitar

skiing

Pyrenees

ANDORRA

Marseille

MONACO

casinos

Apennines

cars

SAN MAR

③

Madrid

Barcelona

port

Leaning Tower of Pisa

Rome

Vati

Lisbon

R. Tagus

PORTUGAL

SPAIN

leather goods

beaches

Balearic Islands

cruise ships

Sardinia

Colosseum

sardines

oranges

flamenco dancers

almonds

Strait of Gibraltar

grapes

Tyrrhenian Sea

Sici

②

MOROCCO

ALGERIA

Mediter

TUNISIA

The south of this region lies on the shores of the warm Mediterranean Sea where many people spend their holidays. Southern Europe and Africa are separated by only 15 kilometres (9 miles) of water known as the Strait of Gibraltar, which links the Atlantic Ocean and the Mediterranean Sea. Two of the world's smallest countries, Vatican City and Monaco, are in Southern Europe.

①

A F R

Ⓐ

Ⓑ

Ⓒ

A gondola is a traditional, long, narrow rowing boat used for transport on the canals in Venice.

N
W E
S

POLAND

Warsaw

cathedral

Prague

CZECH REPUBLIC

glass making

Kiev

UKRAINE

brown bears

R. Dniester

Vienna

SLOVAKIA

Bratislava

Carpathian Mts

HUNGARY

Budapest

MOLDOVA

Chisinau

Hungarian church

SLOVENIA

Ljubljana

Zagreb

CROATIA

castle

ROMANIA

Croatian house

Belgrade

Bucharest

BOSNIA-HERZEGOVINA

R. Danube

roses

Sarajevo

SERBIA

Balkan Mts

grapes

MONTENEGRO

Priština

Sofia

Black Sea

Podgorica

KOSOVO

Skopje

BULGARIA

Adriatic Sea

Tirana

ALBANIA

MACEDONIA

Istanbul

pizza

Naples

Greek pottery

fortress

spaghetti

olives

Greek church

GREECE

Aegean Sea

TURKEY

Izmir

Parthenon

Athens

kebabs

Ionian Sea

volcano

Valletta

MALTA

Cretan mosque

Crete

fishing boats

Knossos

Did you know?

• In France April Fool's Day is known as April Fish Day.

Try this!

Many famous buidings and ruins are found in this region.
Look at the map and find

Arc de Triomphe
Colosseum
Knossos
Parthenon
Leaning Tower of Pisa

LIBYA

AFRICA

EGYPT

D E F

29

Asia

Asia is the largest continent. It is bigger than Europe and Africa combined. Asia extends from the Ural mountains to the Pacific Ocean in the east and from the Arctic Ocean to the Indian Ocean in the south. Climates vary from the cold Arctic in the north to hot tropical in the south.

Arctic

EUROPE

Moscow

Ural Mountains

S   i

RUSSIAN FEDERATION

④

Black Sea

CYPRUS

TURKEY

Ankara

GEORGIA

T'bilisi

Yerevan

AZERBAIJAN

Baku

ARMENIA

Caspian Sea

Astana

UZBEKISTAN

KAZAKHSTAN

Bishkek

KYRGYZSTAN

LEBANON

ISRAEL

SYRIA

Damascus

Amman

Baghdad

TURKMENISTAN

Ashgabat

Tehran

Tashkent

Dushanbe

TAJIKISTAN

Kunlun Shan

③

JORDAN

IRAQ

Kuwait

KUWAIT

IRAN

AFGHANISTAN

Kabul

Islamabad

Plateau of Tibet

Himalaya

BAHRAIN

SAUDI ARABIA

Riyadh

QATAR

The Gulf

Red Sea

UNITED ARAB EMIRATES

Muscat

PAKISTAN

New Delhi

NEPAL

Kathmandu

Mount Everest

BHUTAN

Thimphu

Dhaka

MYANMAR (BURMA)

AFRICA

②

San'a

OMAN

YEMEN

INDIA

BANGLADESH

Naypyidaw

Try this!

This country is also an island. Can you name it?

Socotra (Yemen)

Arabian Sea

Bay of Bengal

Yango (Rango

Andaman Is (India)

N

SRI LANKA

Nicobar Is (India)

W   E

MALDIVES

Sri Jayewardenepura Kotte

①

Answers at the back of the atlas.

S

Indian Ocean

Ocean

Bering
Sea

Sea of
Okhotsk

Where in the world is Asia?

Lake
Baikal

Sea
of
Japan
(East Sea)

Ulan Bator

JAPAN

NGOLIA

NORTH KOREA

Tokyo

Pyongyang

Beijing

Seoul

SOUTH KOREA

CHINA

*East
China
Sea*

Chang Jiang

P a c i f i c

O c e a n

Hanoi

LAOS

Vientiane

*South
China
Sea*

Manila

PALAU

angkok

CAMBODIA

PHILIPPINES

Melekeok

Phnom Penh

VIETNAM

BRUNEI

THAILAND

**Bandar Seri
Begawan**

**Kuala
umpur**

MALAYSIA

Borneo

rajaya

Singapore

SINGAPORE

INDONESIA

EAST TIMOR

O C E A N I A

Jakarta

Dili

Ⓓ

Ⓔ

Ⓕ

Facts

- Area: 45 036 492 square kilometres
  (17 388 686 square miles)

- Largest country: Russian Federation
  17 075 400 square kilometres
  (6 592 849 square miles)

- Longest river: Chang Jiang
  6380 kilometres (3964 miles)

- Highest mountain: Mount Everest
  8848 metres (29 028 feet)

- Largest lake: Caspian Sea
  371 000 square kilometres
  (143 243 square miles)

- Largest island: Borneo
  745 561 square kilometres
  (287 863 square miles)

Did you know?

- The Siberian tiger is the largest living
  cat in the world.

Russian Federation

Arctic Ocean

⑤

Russia is the largest country in the world. It has borders with 14 different countries. Most Russians live in the west of the country. Siberia, in the north, is almost empty. It is dry and extremely cold there. The southwest, on the coast of the Black Sea, is very warm. Much of the country is covered with huge grassy plains, known as steppes.

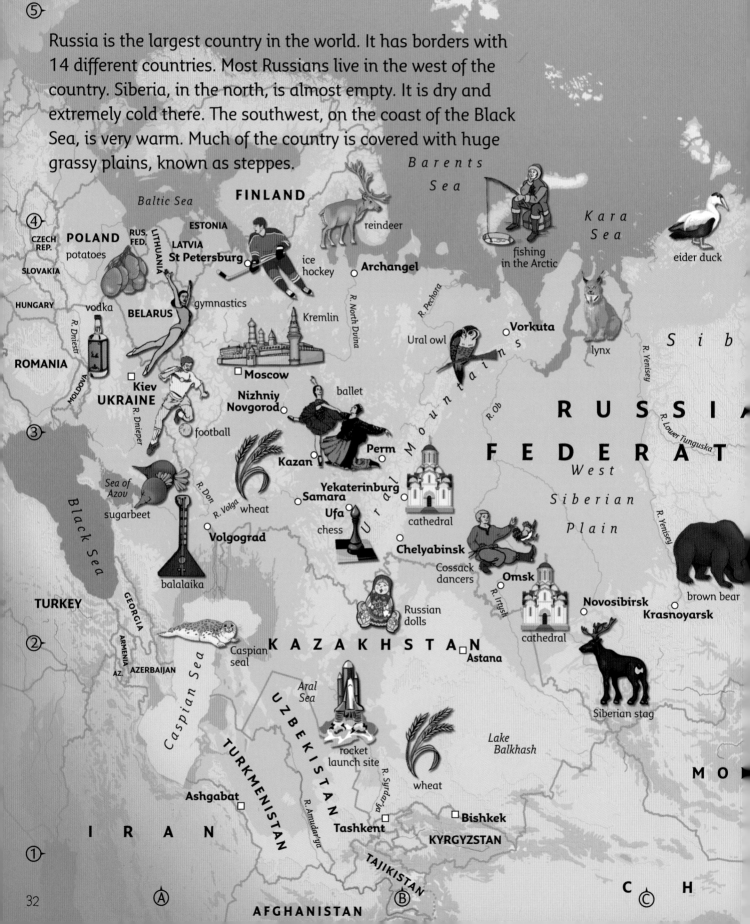

Baltic Sea

FINLAND

Barents Sea

Kara Sea

④

CZECH REP.

POLAND
potatoes

RUS. FED.

LITHUANIA

ESTONIA

LATVIA
St Petersburg

reindeer

fishing in the Arctic

eider duck

SLOVAKIA

ice hockey

Archangel

HUNGARY

vodka

BELARUS

gymnastics

R. North Dvina

R. Pechora

Ural owl

Vorkuta

lynx

S i b

ROMANIA

R. Dniestr

Kremlin

R. Yenisey

MOLDOVA

Kiev
UKRAINE

□

Moscow

Nizhniy Novgorod

ballet

R. Ob

R U S S I A

R. Lower Tunguska

③

R. Dnieper

football

Perm

FEDERAT

West

Sea of Azov

sugarbeet

R. Don

R. Volga

wheat

Kazan

Peкm

Yekaterinburg
Samara

Ufa

chess

cathedral

Siberian

Plain

R. Yenisey

Black Sea

balalaika

Volgograd

Chelyabinsk

Cossack dancers

Omsk

cathedral

Novosibirsk

brown bear

Krasnoyarsk

TURKEY

GEORGIA

②

ARMENIA

AZ. **AZERBAIJAN**

Caspian seal

Caspian Sea

K A Z A K H S T A N

Russian dolls

□
Astana

Siberian stag

Aral Sea

UZBEKISTAN

rocket launch site

R. Syrdar'ya

wheat

Lake Balkhash

M O

I R A N

TURKMENISTAN

R. Amudar'ya

①

Ashgabat
□

Tashkent

□ **Bishkek**

KYRGYZSTAN

TAJIKISTAN

AFGHANISTAN

C H

Ⓒ

Ⓐ

Ⓑ

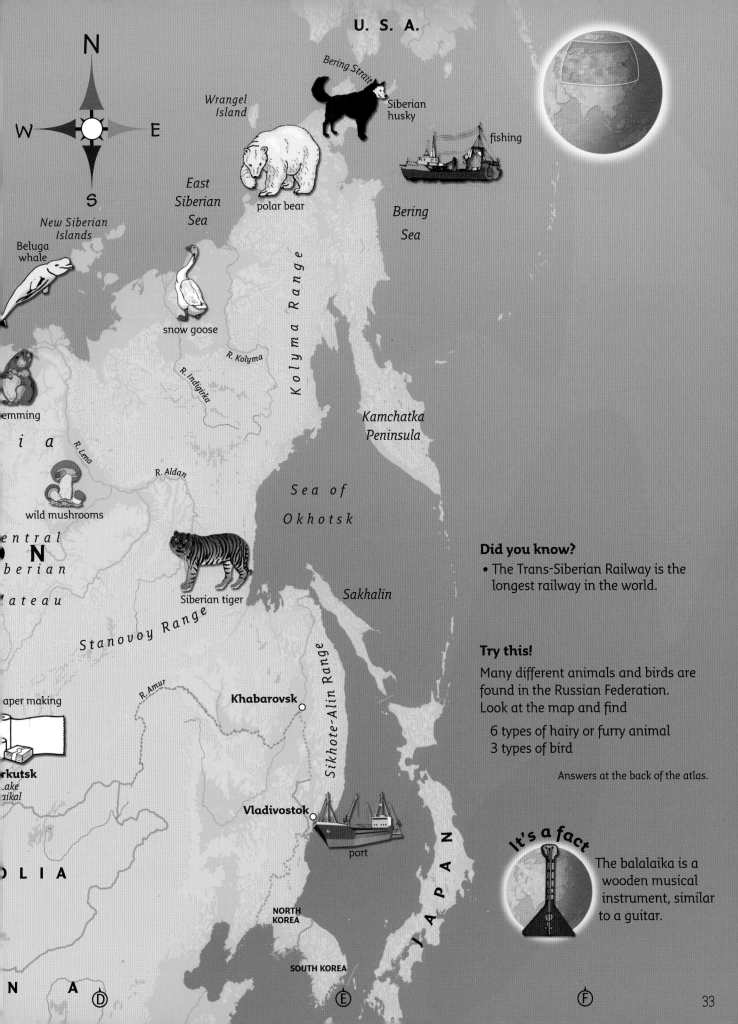

U. S. A.

Bering Strait

Wrangel Island

Siberian husky

fishing

East Siberian Sea

polar bear

Bering Sea

New Siberian Islands

Beluga whale

snow goose

R. Kolyma

R. Indigirka

Kamchatka Peninsula

...emming

R. Lena

R. Aldan

wild mushrooms

Sea of Okhotsk

...ntral

...N

...berian

...ateau

Sakhalin

Siberian tiger

Stanovoy Range

Sikhote-Alin Range

R. Amur

...aper making

Khabarovsk

...rkutsk

...ake ...ikal

Vladivostok

port

NORTH KOREA

SOUTH KOREA

J A P A N

Kolyma Range

Did you know?

• The Trans-Siberian Railway is the longest railway in the world.

Try this!

Many different animals and birds are found in the Russian Federation. Look at the map and find

6 types of hairy or furry animal
3 types of bird

Answers at the back of the atlas.

It's a fact

The balalaika is a wooden musical instrument, similar to a guitar.

Ⓓ   Ⓔ   Ⓕ   33

Southwest Asia

Black Sea

GREECE

RUSSIA

El'brus

GEORGI

kebabs

Ankara

mosque

coffee

ARMEN

Yerev

Taurus Mts

TURKEY

⑤ The north and west of this area is mountainous, with high ranges extending through Turkey into Iran. The Arabian Peninsula between the Red Sea and The Gulf is mostly dry sandy desert. Water is scarce in much of Southwest Asia. Two major rivers are the Tigris and Euphrates.

Crusader castles

cedar trees

Nicosia

CYPRUS

SYRIA

date palms

Mediterranean Sea

Beirut

LEBANON

ISRAEL

Damascus

④ **LIBYA**

Baghd

R. Euphrates

Did you know?
- Damascus, the capital of Syria, is one of the oldest cities in the world.

Amman

JORDAN

Jerusalem

Syrian Desert

oil refineries

IRA

Cairo

Try this!
Look at the map. Can you find these:

Sphinx

R. Nile

Dome of the Rock

③ 3 Arabian animals
1 religious building
1 sport popular in Pakistan

Answers at the back of the atlas.

Arabian fox

An Nafud

carpet

desert safari

Bedouin tent

Arabian headdress

E G Y P T

scuba diving

Najd

Riya

② crocodile

R. Nile

S A U D

Muslim praying at Mecca

angel fish

Asir

Red Sea

Arabian hor

It's a fact
The oryx is a type of antelope with long, straight horns.

S U D A N

dhow

San'a

E R I T R E A

YE

① Ras Dejen

Ⓐ

E T H I O P I A

Ⓑ

DJIBOUTI

Ⓒ G

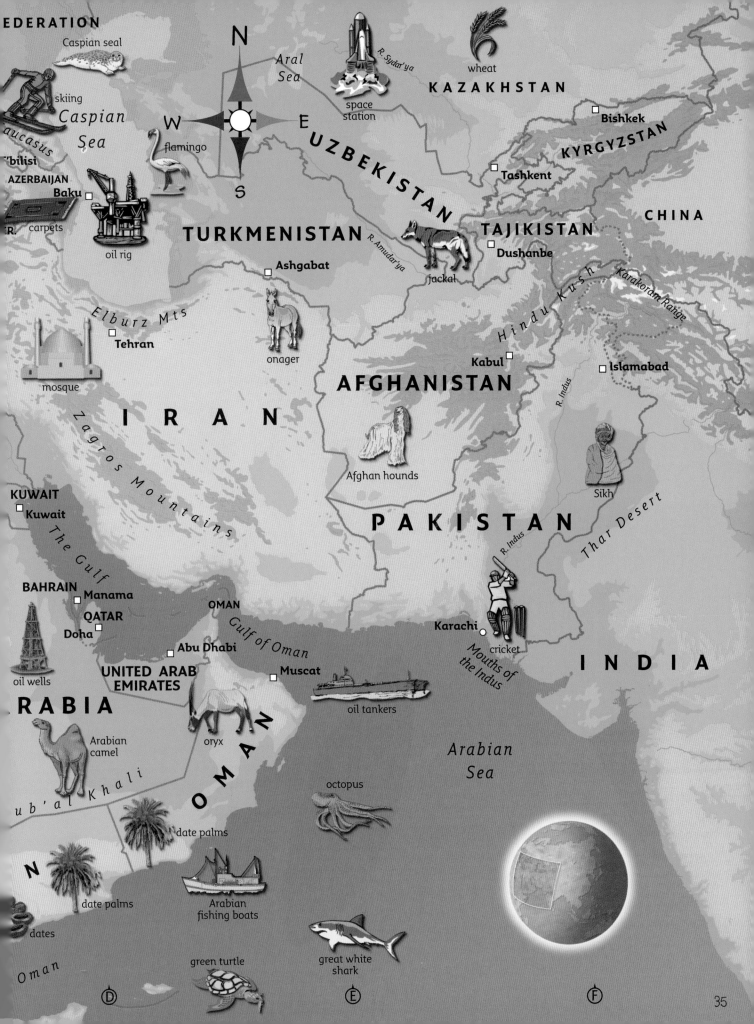

EDERATION

Caspian seal

skiing

Caspian Sea

aucasus

'bilisi

AZERBAIJAN

Baku

R.

carpets

oil rig

flamingo

mosque

Elburz Mts

Tehran

IRAN

Zagros Mountains

KUWAIT

Kuwait

The Gulf

BAHRAIN
Manama

QATAR
Doha

oil wells

UNITED ARAB
EMIRATES

Abu Dhabi

RABIA

Arabian
camel

ub'al Khali

N

date palms

dates

Oman

D

Aral Sea

space station

R. Sydar'ya

wheat

KAZAKHSTAN

Bishkek

KYRGYZSTAN

Tashkent

UZBEKISTAN

TURKMENISTAN

R. Amudar'ya

jackal

Ashgabat

onager

TAJIKISTAN

Dushanbe

Hindu Kush

Karakoram Range

CHINA

Kabul

AFGHANISTAN

Islamabad

R. Indus

Afghan hounds

Sikh

PAKISTAN

Thar Desert

R. Indus

OMAN

Gulf of Oman

Muscat

oxyx

OMAN

oil tankers

Karachi

cricket

Mouths of
the Indus

INDIA

Arabian Sea

octopus

date palms

Arabian
fishing boats

green turtle

great white
shark

E

F

35

South Asia

⑦ South Asia is a region of contrasting landscapes and weather. In the north is the great mountain range of Himalaya where the climate is harsh and few people live. The lands at the mouths of the Ganges river are low lying and flooding occurs during the heavy rains in the monsoon season. Most people live in the river valleys, plains and big cities.

Try this!

Many different animals, birds and fish are found in this region.
Look at the map and find

3 members of the cat family
2 types of bird
1 type of animal with sharp spines

Answers at the back of the atlas.

N
W ● E
S

C H I N A

Kunlun Shan

Plateau of Tibet

□ Lhasa

Tibetan monks

Thimphu
BHUTAN

Mount Everest

yak

Kathmandu

Nepalese

snow leopard

H i m a l a y a

N E P A L

Indian rhinoceros

Patna

Kashmir stag

K2

elephants

R. Brahmaputra

BANGLADESH

Golden Temple, Amritsar

Delhi
New Delhi

Taj Mahal

Jaipur

TAJIKISTAN

□ Dushanbe

mountain goat

H i n d u   K u s h

Islamabad □

Kabul □

Lahore ○

AFGHANISTAN

Faisalabad ○

Sikh

Thar Desert

P A K I S T A N

R. Indus

⑥ jackal

⑤ Afghan hound

36

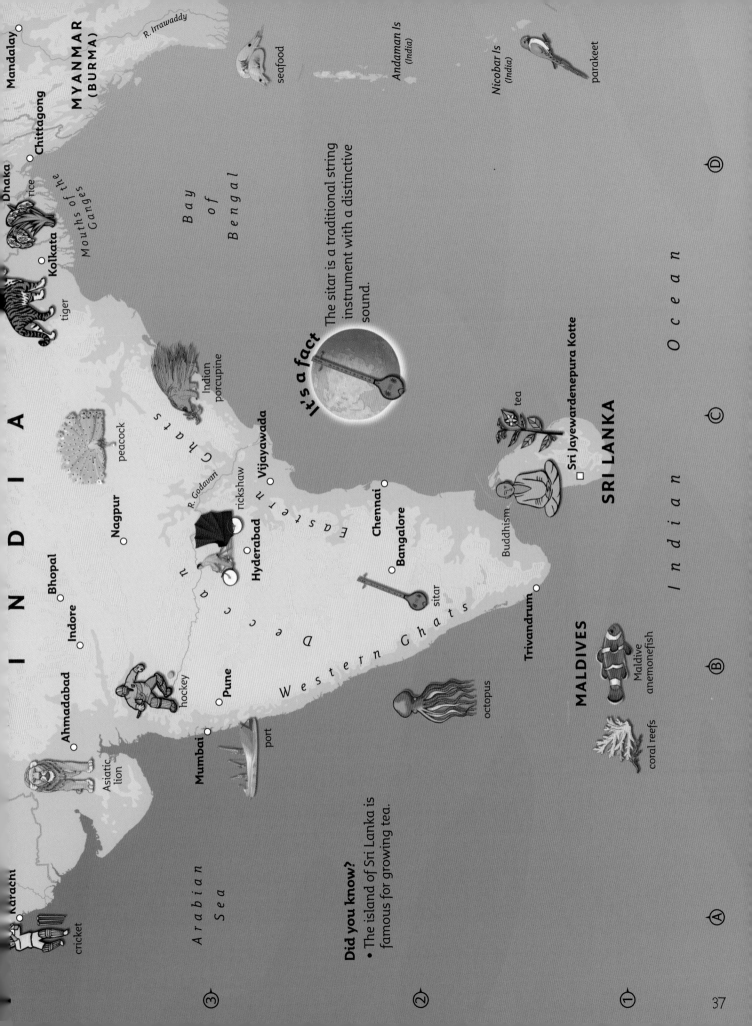

Karachi

cricket

Ahmadabad

Asiatic lion

Indore

Bhopal

Mumbai

port

hockey

I N D I A

Nagpur

Pune

peacock

Indian porcupine

R. Godavari

Western Ghats

rickshaw

Vijayawada

Hyderabad

Eastern Ghats

Chennai

Bangalore

sitar

octopus

Trivandrum

MALDIVES

Maldive anemonefish

coral reefs

Arabian Sea

Did you know?
• The island of Sri Lanka is famous for growing tea.

It's a fact

The sitar is a traditional string instrument with a distinctive sound.

tiger

Kolkata

Mouths of the Ganges

rice

Dhaka

Chittagong

Mandalay

MYANMAR (BURMA)

R. Irrawaddy

seafood

Andaman Is (India)

Nicobar Is (India)

parakeet

Bay of Bengal

Buddhism

tea

Sri Jayewardenepura Kotte

SRI LANKA

Indian Ocean

A   B   C   D

1   2   3

China and Japan

⑤

W N E S

KAZAKHSTAN

MONGOLIA

□ **Ulan Bator**

Hulur Nur

Mongolian dancers

KYRGYZSTAN

④

Tien Shan

Bosten Hu

Gobi Desert

Bactrian camel

Forbidd City

Huang He

Beijin

Kunlun Shan

Great Wall

terracotta soldier

Pekinese do

③

snow leopard

Plateau of Tibet

Himalaya

yak

C H I N A

Xi'an

bowl of rice

Chinese vase

Chang Jiang

Wul

chrysanthemum

Chongqing

NEPAL

Mount Everest

②

BHUTAN

INDIA

China is a land of high mountains, empty deserts, lush valleys and busy cities. Japan is made up of 4 big islands and over 3500 smaller ones. Lots of people live and work in its big cities. Japan is a hotspot for earthquakes and volcanoes.

giant panda

bamboo

firework

Guangzhou

Ho Ko

gymnastics

VIETNAM

①

MYANMAR

LAOS

Bay of Bengal

Gulf of Tongking

Hainan

38

Ⓐ

Ⓑ

Ⓒ

RUSSIAN FEDERATION

sperm whale
Sea of Okhotsk

skiing

Sapporo

JAPAN

Lake Khanka

Harbin

kites

bonsai tree

Sea of Japan (East Sea)

Shenyang

NORTH KOREA

Buddhist monk
anjin

karate

Pyongyang

Korea Bay

Seoul

SOUTH KOREA

sumo wrestling

girl in kimono

Tokyo

Honshu

electronics industry

bullet train

rice growing

Yellow Sea

car industry

rickshaw

Shanghai

Sakura-jima

puffer fish

East China Sea

chopsticks

Ryukyu Islands

tea

octopus

Chinese junk

T'aipei

pagoda

Taiwan

tuna

Pacific Ocean

port

th Sea

Ⓓ

PHILIPPINES

Ⓔ

Did you know?
• Japan has about 1500 earthquakes each year.

Try this!
China has many different animals.
Look at the map and find

The big furry animal who loves to eat bamboo.

Many sports are played in Japan

Can you name 2 of these?

Answers at the back of the atlas.

It's a fact

Each year a panda can eat 5 tonnes of bamboo.

Southeast Asia

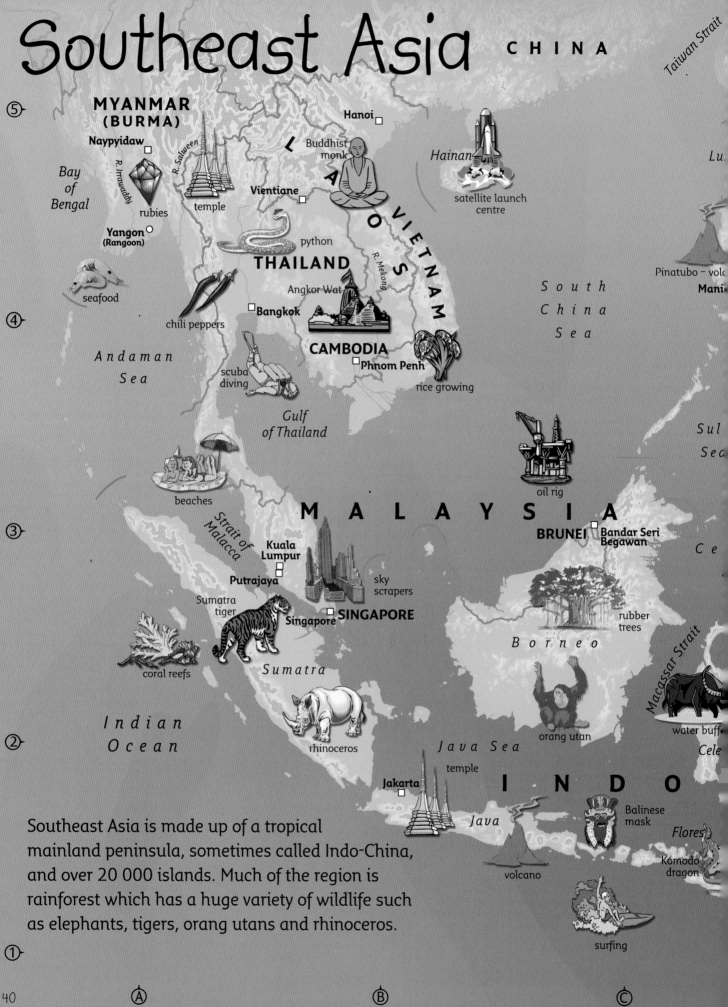

CHINA

Taiwan Strait

MYANMAR (BURMA)

Naypyidaw

R. Salween

Bay of Bengal

R. Irrawaddy

rubies

temple

Yangon (Rangoon)

Vientiane

L A O S

Hanoi

Buddhist monk

Hainan

satellite launch centre

Lu

seafood

python

THAILAND

Angkor Wat

R. Mekong

V I E T N A M

South China Sea

Pinatubo - vol

Mani

chili peppers

Bangkok

Andaman Sea

scuba diving

CAMBODIA

Phnom Penh

rice growing

Sul Sea

Gulf of Thailand

beaches

oil rig

M A L A Y S I A

BRUNEI Bandar Seri Begawan

Ce

Strait of Malacca

Kuala Lumpur

Putrajaya

sky scrapers

Sumatra tiger

Singapore **SINGAPORE**

rubber trees

Borneo

Macassar Strait

coral reefs

Sumatra

orang utan

water buff

Indian Ocean

rhinoceros

Java Sea

temple

Cele

Jakarta

I N D O

Balinese mask

Flores

Java

volcano

Komodo dragon

Southeast Asia is made up of a tropical mainland peninsula, sometimes called Indo-China, and over 20 000 islands. Much of the region is rainforest which has a huge variety of wildlife such as elephants, tigers, orang utans and rhinoceros.

surfing

40

Ⓐ   Ⓑ   Ⓒ

⑤ ④ ③ ② ①

tuna

P a c i f i c

O c e a n

trait

uzon

PHILIPPINES

oyster and pearl

Mindanao

pineapples

e s

Molucca Sea

clams

coral reefs

coconut
palm tree

E S I A

B a n d a   S e a

cowrie shell

Dili

**EAST
TIMOR**

A r a f u r a

S e a

□ **Melekeok**

PALAU

manta
ray

Puncak Jaya

N e w

G u i n e a

PAPUA NEW

GUINEA

rubber trees

C o r a l

S e a

Did you know?
• The Sumatran tiger is the smallest
tiger. It is a very fast swimmer.

Try this!
2 water sports are shown on the map.
Can you name them?

Answers at the back of the atlas.

Ⓓ   **A U S T R A L I A**   Ⓔ   Ⓕ   41

Oceania

⑤

N W E S

FEDERATED STATES OF MICRONESIA

INDONESIA

Puncak Jaya ▲

New Guinea

PAPUA NEW GUINEA

Solomon Sea

Arafura Sea

Port Moresby

Honiar

④

Timor Sea

Gulf of Carpentaria

Coral Sea

Indian Ocean

Great Sandy Desert

Great Barrier Reef

Great Dividing Range

AUSTRALIA

Lake Eyre

③

Great Victoria Desert

R. Darling

Great Dividing Range

Great Australian Bight

R. Murray

Great Dividing **Canberra**

Tasman Sea

Tasmania

②

Oceania is the smallest continent and lies within the
tropics. It is made up of the countries of Australia, New
Zealand, Papua New Guinea and over 20 000 small Pacific
islands. Australia is by far the largest country and the
majority of the population live on the coast. The central
region of the country is a vast desert known as the outback.
New Zealand is mountainous with a temperate climate and
Papua New Guinea is mainly rainforest.

①

Ⓐ Ⓑ Ⓒ

Bairiki

Yaren

KIRIBATI

NAURU

SOLOMON
ISLANDS

TUVALU

Vaiaku

VANUATU

Wallis and
Futuna Islands
(France)

SAMOA

Apia

Port Vila

American
Samoa
(USA)

Suva

TONGA

FRENCH
POLYNESIA

New
Caledonia
(France)

Nouméa

FIJI

Nuku'alofa

Niue
(New
Zealand)

Cook
Islands
(New
Zealand)

Did you know?

- Kangaroos are only found in Australia and New Guinea but there are over 40 different types.

Facts

- Area: 8 844 516 square kilometres (3 414 887 square miles)

- Largest country: Australia 7 692 024 square kilometres (2 969 907 square miles)

- Longest river: Murray-Darling 3750 kilometres (2330 miles)

- Highest mountain: Puncak Jaya 5030 metres (16 502 feet)

- Largest lake: Lake Eyre 0-8900 square kilometres (0-3436 square miles)

- Largest island: New Guinea 808 510 square kilometres (312 167 square miles)

Pacific

Ocean

NEW
ZEALAND

*North
Island*

Wellington

*South
Island*

Try this!

Which countries do these flags belong to?

Answers at the back of the atlas.

Australia & New Zealand

INDONESIA

The narrow, fertile coast of eastern Australia is separated from the rest of the country by the Great Dividing Range. The highest mountain in Australia, Mount Kosciuszko, is here. New Zealand is made up of two islands. There are volcanoes on North Island. South Island has snowy mountains and glaciers.

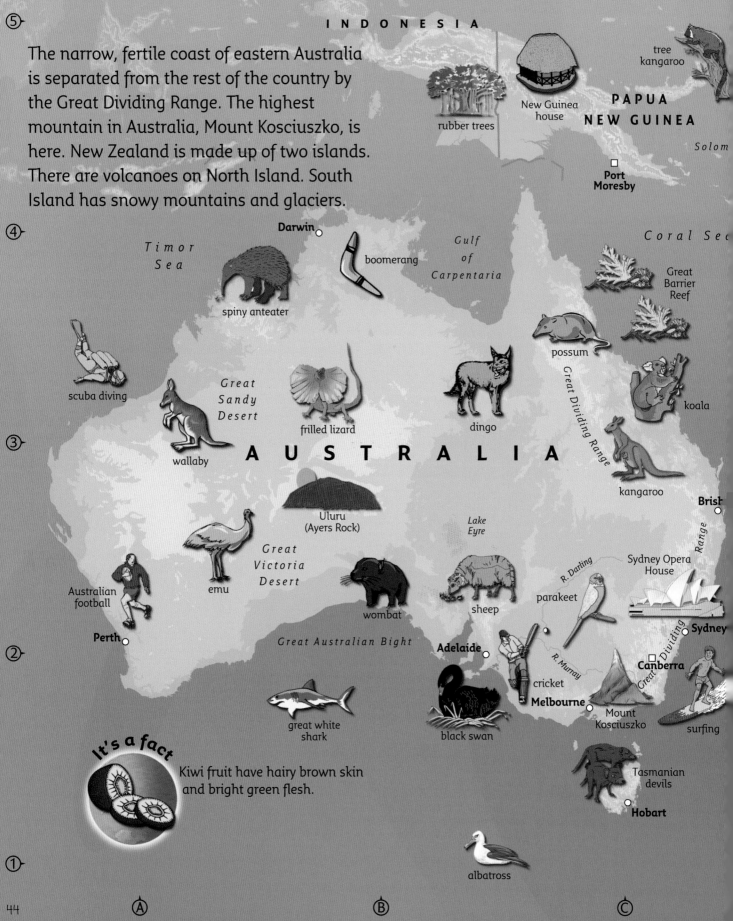

rubber trees

New Guinea house

tree kangaroo

PAPUA NEW GUINEA

Solom

□ Port Moresby

④

Darwin ○

Timor Sea

boomerang

Gulf of Carpentaria

Coral Sea

Great Barrier Reef

spiny anteater

possum

scuba diving

Great Sandy Desert

frilled lizard

dingo

Great Dividing Range

koala

wallaby

A U S T R A L I A

kangaroo

③

Brisb ○

Uluru (Ayers Rock)

Lake Eyre

Range

emu

Great Victoria Desert

wombat

sheep

R. Darling

parakeet

Sydney Opera House

Australian football

Perth ○

Great Australian Bight

Adelaide ○

cricket

R. Murray

Great Dividing

Sydney

②

□ Canberra

Melbourne ○

Mount Kosciuszko

surfing

great white shark

black swan

Tasmanian devils

It's a fact

Kiwi fruit have hairy brown skin and bright green flesh.

Hobart

①

albatross

Ⓐ   Ⓑ   Ⓒ

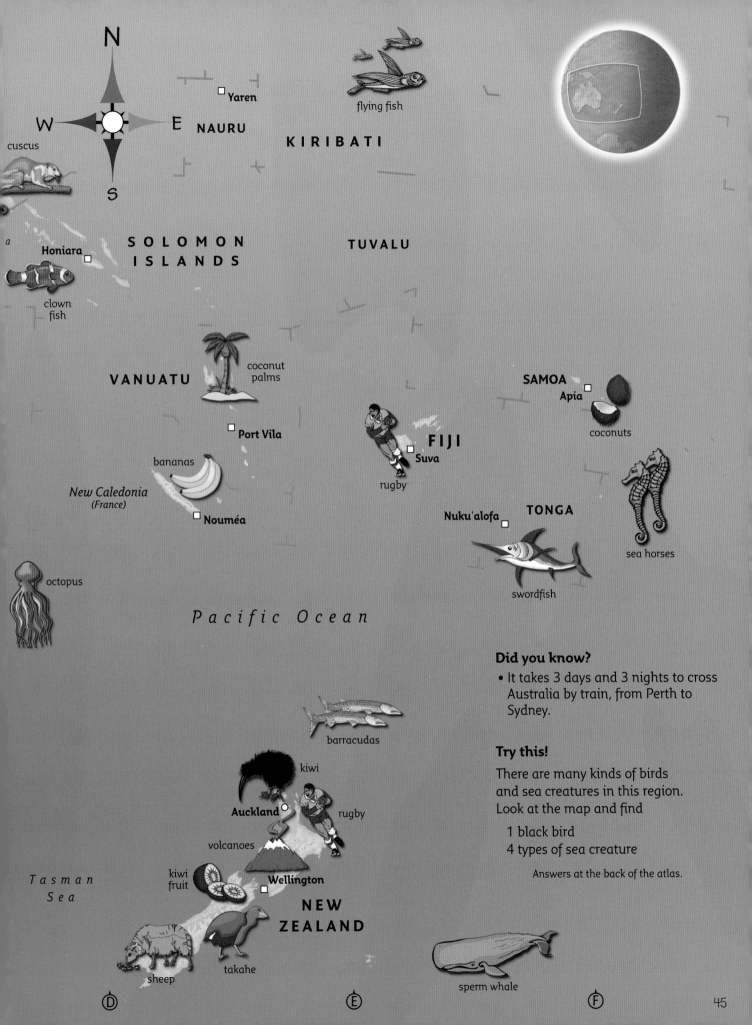

N
W E
S

cuscus

Yaren
NAURU

KIRIBATI

flying fish

a

SOLOMON
ISLANDS

Honiara

clown
fish

TUVALU

coconut
palms

VANUATU

SAMOA
Apia

coconuts

Port Vila

bananas

New Caledonia
(France)

FIJI
Suva

rugby

sea horses

Nouméa

Nuku'alofa **TONGA**

octopus

swordfish

Pacific Ocean

Did you know?

• It takes 3 days and 3 nights to cross Australia by train, from Perth to Sydney.

barracudas

kiwi

Auckland
rugby

volcanoes

kiwi
fruit

Tasman
Sea

Wellington

NEW
ZEALAND

sheep   takahe

sperm whale

Try this!

There are many kinds of birds and sea creatures in this region. Look at the map and find

1 black bird
4 types of sea creature

Answers at the back of the atlas.

The Arctic Ocean

The Arctic Ocean is at the North Pole. Much of the sea is covered in ice all year round. It is the smallest and shallowest ocean in the world.

Try this!

Look at the map and find

1 type of air transport
1 type of water transport
1 type of land transport

Answers at the back of the atlas.

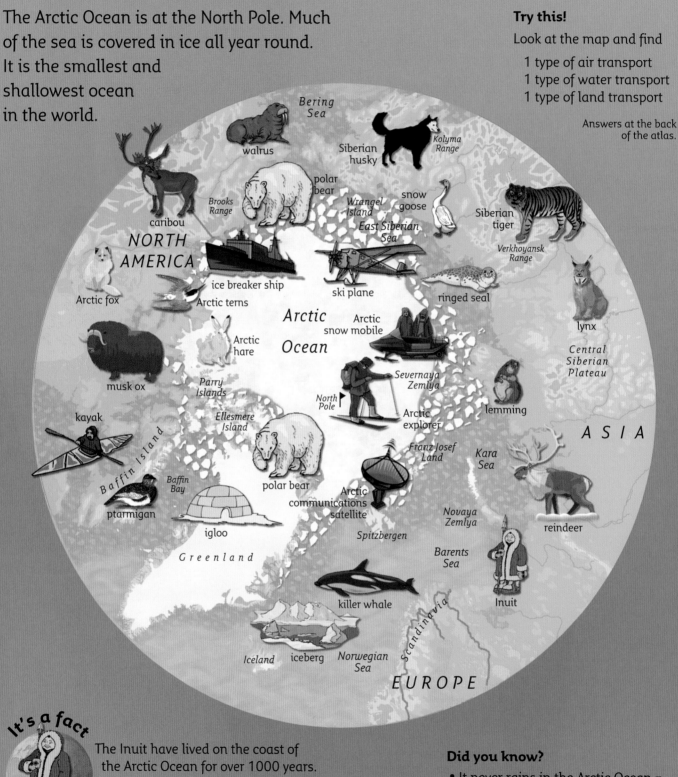

Bering Sea

walrus

Siberian husky

Kolyma Range

polar bear

snow goose

Siberian tiger

caribou

Brooks Range

Wrangel Island

East Siberian Sea

Verkhoyansk Range

NORTH AMERICA

ice breaker ship

ski plane

ringed seal

Arctic fox

Arctic terns

Arctic Ocean

Arctic snow mobile

lynx

Arctic hare

musk ox

Parry Islands

Severnaya Zemlya

Central Siberian Plateau

North Pole

Arctic explorer

lemming

kayak

Ellesmere Island

ASIA

Baffin Island

Baffin Bay

polar bear

Arctic communications satellite

Franz Josef Land

Kara Sea

ptarmigan

igloo

Spitzbergen

Novaya Zemlya

reindeer

Greenland

Barents Sea

Inuit

killer whale

Scandinavia

Iceland

iceberg

Norwegian Sea

EUROPE

It's a fact

The Inuit have lived on the coast of the Arctic Ocean for over 1000 years.

Did you know?
• It never rains in the Arctic Ocean – it only snows.

46

Antarctica

Antarctica is the area of thick ice surrounding the South Pole. It is the coldest, windiest and driest continent.

albatross

blue whale

cruise ship

South Orkney Islands

South Shetland Islands

Weddell Sea

Enderby Land

Queen Maud Land

Adelie penguin

Kemp Land

Graham Land

Antarctic Peninsula

iceberg

Palmer Land

Alexander Island

Berkner Island

weather balloon

fur seal

Prydz Bay

ANTARCTICA

Bellingshausen Sea

chin strap penguin

South Pole

polar explorers

Ellsworth Land

snow mobile

Southern Ocean

glacier

Mary Byrd Land

Queen Mary Land

elephant seal

Amundsen Sea

Ross Ice Shelf

Wilkes Land

Transantarctic Mountains

ski plane

emperor penguins

Ross Sea

Oates Land

Southern Ocean

killer whale

Did you know?
• No one country owns Antarctica.

Where have you been?

This world map shows some of the most visited countries in the world. You may have also visited some of these places. Perhaps you spent a holiday or visited friends and relations in these countries.

Look at the comments from children who have spent some time travelling in far away places. Would you agree with their comments or have you more interesting stories to tell?

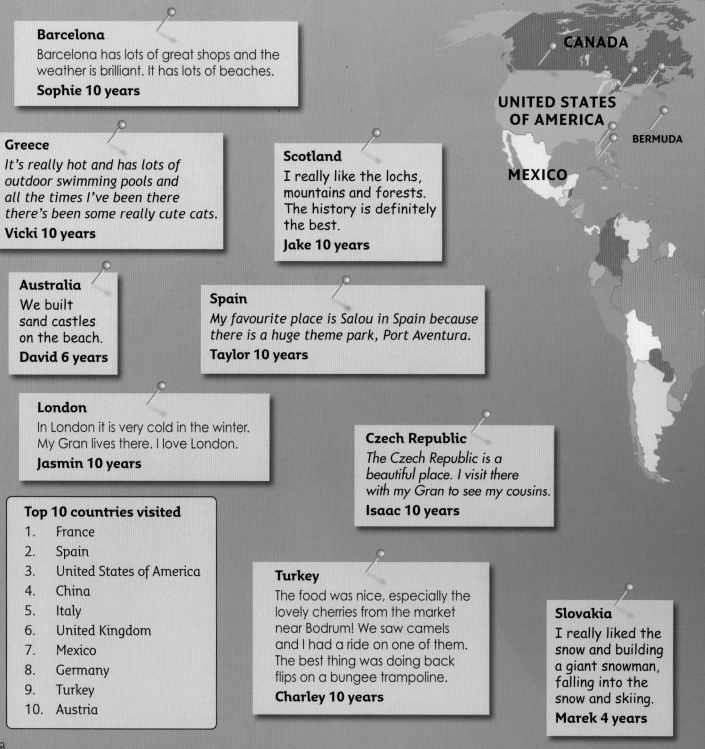

Barcelona

Barcelona has lots of great shops and the weather is brilliant. It has lots of beaches.

Sophie 10 years

Greece

It's really hot and has lots of outdoor swimming pools and all the times I've been there there's been some really cute cats.

Vicki 10 years

Scotland

I really like the lochs, mountains and forests. The history is definitely the best.

Jake 10 years

Australia

We built sand castles on the beach.

David 6 years

Spain

My favourite place is Salou in Spain because there is a huge theme park, Port Aventura.

Taylor 10 years

London

In London it is very cold in the winter. My Gran lives there. I love London.

Jasmin 10 years

Czech Republic

The Czech Republic is a beautiful place. I visit there with my Gran to see my cousins.

Isaac 10 years

CANADA

UNITED STATES OF AMERICA

BERMUDA

MEXICO

Top 10 countries visited
1. France
2. Spain
3. United States of America
4. China
5. Italy
6. United Kingdom
7. Mexico
8. Germany
9. Turkey
10. Austria

Turkey

The food was nice, especially the lovely cherries from the market near Bodrum! We saw camels and I had a ride on one of them. The best thing was doing back flips on a bungee trampoline.

Charley 10 years

Slovakia

I really liked the snow and building a giant snowman, falling into the snow and skiing.

Marek 4 years

What do you think?

France
I was in France whilst they were in the final of the World Cup. I got to stay up late and make as much noise as I could without being heard.
Calum 10 years

Portugal
I like the swimming pools outside.
Cain 10 years

France
I used to live in France. I will always have this memory. One day it went snowy, sun, snow, sun etc....
Cameron 10 years

GERMANY
UNITED KINGDOM
CZECH REP.
IRELAND
SLOVAKIA
FRANCE
AUSTRIA
ITALY
PORTUGAL
SPAIN
GREECE
TURKEY

CHINA

INDIA

Scotland
The most exciting thing was when I was panning for gold at the Wanlockhead Lead Mine Museum and found some in the bottom of my pan.
Callum 8 years

MALAYSIA

KENYA

AUSTRALIA

SOUTH AFRICA

Florida
We went to Disneyworld to see Mickey Mouse. It was very hot.
Brad 7 years

NEW ZEALAND

Majorca
It is famous because it has a Pirate Show. Its main place is Palma.
Ross 10 years

Scotland
I went to Millport. It was thunder and lightning. It struck a lamppost and it fell down on the road.
Antonio 10 years

Scotland
My favourite place is Loch Lomond.
Jordan 10 years

Scotland
Edinburgh Dungeons has the most scary weirdest monsters in the world. I got the monster stuck in my dreams.
Brian 10 years

Disneyland Paris
Disneyland was great. It was sad when I had to leave.
Daniel 10 years

Spain
I liked Majorca because of the sun and the price of shopping. It was also really good because of the big beaches.
Kieran 10 years

Where have you been?

There are many reasons to travel to far away places. The symbols around this map show a selection of these. Names on the map tell us some of the best places to visit.

More interesting stories are also shown.

Sightseeing

Beach holiday

North America

Rocky Mountains

Winter sports

Caribbean Sea   Cruise

South America

Andes

Bird watching

S a

Desert Safar

Exploring

A n t

USA
I like Universal Studio because it has fantastic rides. I would give it a ten out of ten.
Sam 10 years

Kenya
We were in a big car and saw elephants and lions. I liked the lions but they had big teeth. It was very dusty and hot.
Katie 7 years

USA
I used to live in Vermont. In winter it snows a lot and in the summer it is very hot.
Aidan 10 years

India
India is the greatest place ever.
Naomi 10 years

Malaysia
We went to the jungle and saw lots of animals in the trees. I was scared because the animals made lots of noise at night. It was hot but it rained every day.
Kim 8 years

Australia
I love Australia because of all the different animals on land and in the water and all of the lovely weather.
Robbie 10 years

Canary Islands
My favourite place is Tenerife because it's very comfortable...
Darren 10 years

Cadiz, Spain
My feet were almost burnt when I went on the beaches because the sand was so hot. Luckily the water cooled me down.
Helen 10 years

What do you think?

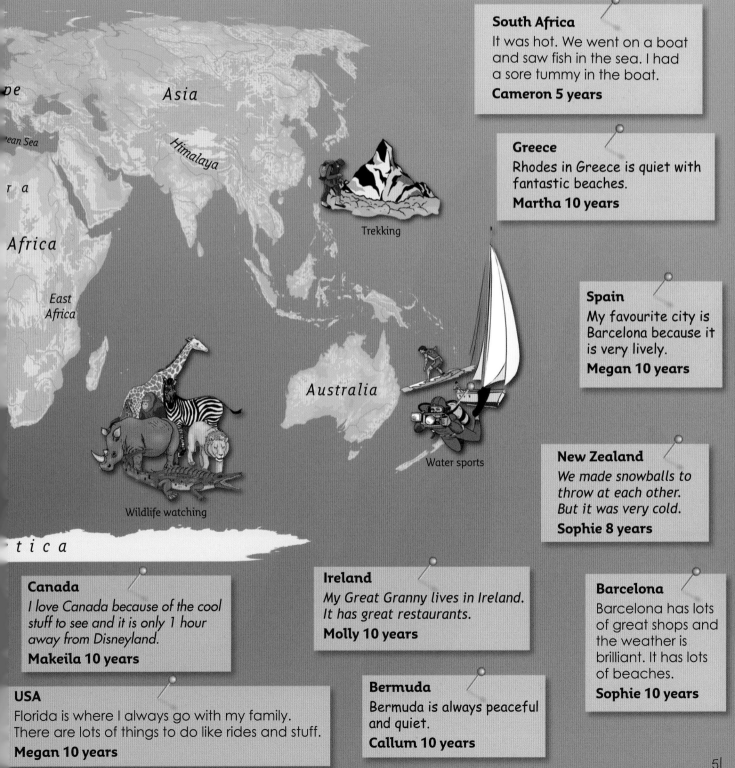

Turkey
It's really HOT!! I sleep walked into the hallway of our dormitory and I had nightmares about one of my Aunt's friend's cousins.
Sean 10 years

Scotland
Arran is an island off the southwest coast of Scotland. The funniest thing is when my friend catapults people across the bedroom with his feet. The best thing was when I got to ride a horse through a river on a pony trek.
Rona 10 years

South Africa
It was hot. We went on a boat and saw fish in the sea. I had a sore tummy in the boat.
Cameron 5 years

Greece
Rhodes in Greece is quiet with fantastic beaches.
Martha 10 years

Spain
My favourite city is Barcelona because it is very lively.
Megan 10 years

New Zealand
We made snowballs to throw at each other. But it was very cold.
Sophie 8 years

Canada
I love Canada because of the cool stuff to see and it is only 1 hour away from Disneyland.
Makeila 10 years

Ireland
My Great Granny lives in Ireland. It has great restaurants.
Molly 10 years

Barcelona
Barcelona has lots of great shops and the weather is brilliant. It has lots of beaches.
Sophie 10 years

USA
Florida is where I always go with my family. There are lots of things to do like rides and stuff.
Megan 10 years

Bermuda
Bermuda is always peaceful and quiet.
Callum 10 years

Asia

Himalaya

Trekking

Africa

East Africa

Australia

Water sports

Wildlife watching

Countries of the World

Flag	COUNTRY, CONTINENT / Capital City / Population	Area square kilometres (square miles)
	AFGHANISTAN, ASIA — **Kabul** — 28 150 000	652 225 (251 825)
	ALBANIA, EUROPE — **Tirana** — 3 155 000	28 748 (11 100)
	ALGERIA, AFRICA — **Algiers** — 34 895 000	2 381 741 (919 595)
	ANGOLA, AFRICA — **Luanda** — 18 498 000	1 246 700 (481 353)
	ARGENTINA, SOUTH AMERICA — **Buenos Aires** — 40 276 000	2 766 889 (1 068 302)
	ARMENIA, ASIA — **Yerevan** — 3 083 000	29 800 (11 506)
	AUSTRALIA, OCEANIA — **Canberra** — 21 293 000	7 692 024 (2 969 907)
	AUSTRIA, EUROPE — **Vienna** — 8 364 000	83 855 (32 377)
	BAHRAIN, ASIA — **Manama** — 791 000	691 (267)
	BANGLADESH, ASIA — **Dhaka** — 162 221 000	143 998 (55 598)
	BELARUS, EUROPE — **Minsk** — 9 634 000	207 600 (80 155)
	BELGIUM, EUROPE — **Brussels** — 10 647 000	30 520 (11 784)
	BENIN, AFRICA — **Porto Novo** — 8 935 000	112 620 (43 483)
	BHUTAN, ASIA — **Thimphu** — 697 000	46 620 (18 000)
	BOLIVIA, SOUTH AMERICA — **La Paz/Sucre** — 9 863 000	1 098 581 (424 164)
	BOSNIA-HERZEGOVINA, EUROPE — **Sarajevo** — 3 767 000	51 130 (19 741)
	BOTSWANA, AFRICA — **Gaborone** — 1 950 000	581 370 (224 468)
	BRAZIL, SOUTH AMERICA — **Brasília** — 193 734 000	8 514 879 (3 287 613)
	BRUNEI, ASIA — **Bandar Seri Begawan** — 400 000	5 765 (2 226)
	BULGARIA, EUROPE — **Sofia** — 7 545 000	110 994 (42 855)
	BURKINA FASO, AFRICA — **Ouagadougou** — 15 757 000	274 200 (105 869)
	BURUNDI, AFRICA — **Bujumbura** — 8 303 000	27 835 (10 747)
	CAMBODIA, ASIA — **Phnom Penh** — 14 805 000	181 035 (69 884)
	CAMEROON, AFRICA — **Yaoundé** — 19 522 000	475 442 (183 569)
	CANADA, NORTH AMERICA — **Ottawa** — 33 573 000	9 984 670 (3 855 103)
	CENTRAL AFRICAN REPUBLIC, AFRICA — **Bangui** — 4 422 000	622 436 (240 324)
	CHAD, AFRICA — **Ndjamena** — 11 206 000	1 284 000 (495 755)
	CHILE, SOUTH AMERICA — **Santiago** — 16 970 000	756 945 (292 258)
	CHINA, ASIA — **Beijing** — 1 353 123 000	9 620 671 (3 715 979)
	COLOMBIA, SOUTH AMERICA — **Bogotá** — 45 660 000	1 141 748 (440 831)
	CONGO, AFRICA — **Brazzaville** — 3 683 000	342 000 (132 047)
	CONGO, DEMOCRATIC REPUBLIC OF THE, AFRICA — **Kinshasa** — 66 020 000	2 345 410 (905 568)
	COSTA RICA, NORTH AMERICA — **San José** — 4 579 000	51 100 (19 730)
	CÔTE D'IVOIRE, AFRICA — **Yamoussoukro** — 21 075 000	322 463 (124 504)
	CROATIA, EUROPE — **Zagreb** — 4 416 000	56 538 (21 829)
	CUBA, NORTH AMERICA — **Havana** — 11 204 000	110 860 (42 803)
	CYPRUS, ASIA — **Nicosia** — 871 000	9 251 (3 572)
	CZECH REPUBLIC, EUROPE — **Prague** — 10 369 000	78 864 (30 450)
	DENMARK, EUROPE — **Copenhagen** — 5 470 000	43 075 (16 631)

DJIBOUTI, AFRICA	Djibouti	23 200	
	864 000	(8 958)	
DOMINICAN REPUBLIC, NORTH AMERICA	Santo Domingo	48 442	
	10 090 000	(18 704)	
EAST TIMOR, ASIA	Dili	14 874	
	1 134 000	(5 743)	
ECUADOR, SOUTH AMERICA	Quito	272 045	
	13 625 000	(105 037)	
EGYPT, AFRICA	Cairo	1 001 450	
	82 999 000	(386 810)	
EL SALVADOR, NORTH AMERICA	San Salvador	21 041	
	6 163 000	(8 124)	
ERITREA, AFRICA	Asmara	117 400	
	5 073 000	(45 328)	
ESTONIA, EUROPE	Tallinn	45 200	
	1 340 000	(17 452)	
ETHIOPIA, AFRICA	Addis Ababa	1 133 880	
	82 825 000	(437 794)	
FINLAND, EUROPE	Helsinki	338 145	
	5 326 000	(130 559)	
FRANCE, EUROPE	Paris	543 965	
	62 343 000	(210 026)	
GABON, AFRICA	Libreville	267 667	
	1 475 000	(103 347)	
GEORGIA, ASIA	T'bilisi	69 700	
	4 260 000	(26 911)	
GERMANY, EUROPE	Berlin	357 022	
	82 167 000	(137 849)	
GHANA, AFRICA	Accra	238 537	
	23 837 000	(92 100)	
GREECE, EUROPE	Athens	131 957	
	11 161 000	(50 949)	
GUATEMALA, NORTH AMERICA	Guatemala City	108 890	
	14 027 000	(42 043)	
GUINEA, AFRICA	Conakry	245 857	
	10 069 000	(94 926)	
GUINEA-BISSAU, AFRICA	Bissau	36 125	
	1 611 000	(13 948)	
GUYANA, SOUTH AMERICA	Georgetown	214 969	
	762 000	(83 000)	

HAITI, NORTH AMERICA	Port-au-Prince	27 750	
	10 033 000	(10 714)	
HONDURAS, NORTH AMERICA	Tegucigalpa	112 088	
	7 466 000	(43 277)	
HUNGARY, EUROPE	Budapest	93 030	
	9 993 000	(35 919)	
ICELAND, EUROPE	Reykjavik	102 820	
	323 000	(39 699)	
INDIA, ASIA	New Delhi	3 064 898	
	1 198 003 000	(1 183 364)	
INDONESIA, ASIA	Jakarta	1 919 445	
	229 965 000	(741 102)	
IRAN, ASIA	Tehran	1 648 000	
	74 196 000	(636 296)	
IRAQ, ASIA	Baghdad	438 317	
	30 747 000	(169 235)	
IRELAND EUROPE	Dublin	70 282	
	4 515 000	(27 136)	
ISRAEL, ASIA	Jerusalem*	20 770	
	7 170 000	(8 019)	
ITALY, EUROPE	Rome	301 245	
	59 870 000	(116 311)	
JAMAICA, NORTH AMERICA	Kingston	10 991	
	2 719 000	(4 244)	
JAPAN, ASIA	Tokyo	377 727	
	127 156 000	(145 841)	
JORDAN, ASIA	Amman	89 206	
	6 316 000	(34 443)	
KAZAKHSTAN, ASIA	Astana	2 717 300	
	15 637 000	(1 049 155)	
KENYA, AFRICA	Nairobi	582 646	
	39 802 000	(224 961)	
KUWAIT, ASIA	Kuwait	17 818	
	2 985 000	(6 880)	
KYRGYZSTAN, ASIA	Bishkek	198 500	
	5 482 000	(76 641)	
LAOS, ASIA	Vientiane	236 800	
	6 320 000	(91 429)	
LATVIA, EUROPE	Riga	64 589	
	2 249 000	(24 947)	

*not internationally recognised

Countries of the World

Country	Capital	Population	Area (sq km)
LEBANON, ASIA	Beirut	4 224 000	10 452 (4 036)
LESOTHO, AFRICA	Maseru	2 067 000	30 355 (11 720)
LIBERIA, AFRICA	Monrovia	3 955 000	111 369 (43 000)
LIBYA, AFRICA	Tripoli	6 420 000	1 759 540 (679 362)
LITHUANIA, EUROPE	Vilnius	3 287 000	65 200 (25 174)
LUXEMBOURG, EUROPE	Luxembourg	486 000	2 586 (998)
MACEDONIA (F.Y.R.O.M.), EUROPE	Skopje	2 042 000	25 713 (9 928)
MADAGASCAR, AFRICA	Antananarivo	19 625 000	587 041 (226 658)
MALAWI, AFRICA	Lilongwe	15 263 000	118 484 (45 747)
MALAYSIA, ASIA	Kuala Lumpur/Putrajaya	27 468 000	332 965 (128 559)
MALI, AFRICA	Bamako	13 010 000	1 240 140 (478 821)
MAURITANIA, AFRICA	Nouakchott	3 291 000	1 030 700 (397 955)
MEXICO, NORTH AMERICA	Mexico City	109 610 000	1 972 545 (761 604)
MOLDOVA, EUROPE	Chisinau	3 604 000	33 700 (13 017)
MONGOLIA, ASIA	Ulan Bator	2 671 000	1 565 000 (604 250)
MONTENEGRO, EUROPE	Podgorica	624 000	13 812 (5333)
MOROCCO, AFRICA	Rabat	31 993 000	446 550 (172 414)
MOZAMBIQUE, AFRICA	Maputo	22 894 000	799 380 (308 642)
MYANMAR (BURMA), ASIA	Naypyidaw	50 020 000	676 577 (261 228)
NAMIBIA, AFRICA	Windhoek	2 171 000	824 292 (318 261)
NEPAL, ASIA	Kathmandu	29 331 000	147 181 (56 827)
NETHERLANDS, EUROPE	Amsterdam/The Hague	16 592 000	41 526 (16 033)
NEW ZEALAND, OCEANIA	Wellington	4 266 000	270 534 (104 454)
NICARAGUA, NORTH AMERICA	Managua	5 743 000	130 000 (50 193)
NIGER, AFRICA	Niamey	15 290 000	1 267 000 (489 191)
NIGERIA, AFRICA	Abuja	154 729 000	923 768 (356 669)
NORTH KOREA, ASIA	Pyongyang	23 906 000	120 538 (46 540)
NORWAY, EUROPE	Oslo	4 812 000	323 878 (125 050)
OMAN, ASIA	Muscat	2 845 000	309 500 (119 499)
PAKISTAN, ASIA	Islamabad	180 808 000	803 940 (310 403)
PANAMA, NORTH AMERICA	Panama City	3 454 000	77 082 (29 762)
PAPUA NEW GUINEA, OCEANIA	Port Moresby	6 732 000	462 840 (178 704)
PARAGUAY, SOUTH AMERICA	Asunción	6 349 000	406 752 (157 048)
PERU, SOUTH AMERICA	Lima	29 165 000	1 285 216 (496 225)
PHILIPPINES, ASIA	Manila	91 983 000	300 000 (115 831)
POLAND, EUROPE	Warsaw	38 074 000	312 683 (120 728)
PORTUGAL, EUROPE	Lisbon	10 707 000	88 940 (34 340)
QATAR, ASIA	Doha	1 409 000	11 437 (4 416)
ROMANIA, EUROPE	Bucharest	21 275 000	237 500 (91 699)
RUSSIAN FEDERATION, EUROPE/ASIA	Moscow	140 874 000	17 075 400 (6 592 849)

SAUDI ARABIA, ASIA	Riyadh	25 721 000	2 200 000 (849 425)
SENEGAL, AFRICA	Dakar	12 534 000	196 720 (75 954)
SERBIA, EUROPE	Belgrade	7 335 000	77 453 (29 916)
SIERRA LEONE, AFRICA	Freetown	5 696 000	71 740 (27 699)
SINGAPORE, ASIA	Singapore	4 737 000	639 (247)
SLOVAKIA, EUROPE	Bratislava	5 406 000	49 035 (18 933)
SLOVENIA, EUROPE	Ljubljana	2 020 000	20 251 (7 819)
SOMALIA, AFRICA	Mogadishu	9 133 000	637 657 (246 201)
SOUTH AFRICA, REPUBLIC OF, AFRICA	Pretoria/Cape Town/Bloemfontein	50 110 000	1 219 090 (470 693)
SOUTH KOREA, ASIA	Seoul	48 333 000	99 274 (38 330)
SOUTH SUDAN, AFRICA	Juba	8 260 490	644 329 (248 871)
SPAIN, EUROPE	Madrid	44 904 000	504 782 (194 897)
SRI LANKA, ASIA	Sri Jayewardenepura Kotte	20 238 000	65 610 (25 332)
SUDAN, AFRICA	Khartoum	36 371 510	1 861 484 (718 997)
SURINAME, SOUTH AMERICA	Paramaribo	520 000	163 820 (63 251)
SWAZILAND, AFRICA	Mbabane	1 185 000	17 364 (6 704)
SWEDEN, EUROPE	Stockholm	9 249 000	449 964 (173 732)
SWITZERLAND, EUROPE	Bern	7 568 000	41 293 (15 943)
SYRIA, ASIA	Damascus	21 906 000	185 180 (71 498)
TAJIKISTAN, ASIA	Dushanbe	6 952 000	143 100 (55 251)
TANZANIA, AFRICA	Dodoma	43 479 000	945 087 (364 900)
THAILAND, ASIA	Bangkok	67 764 000	513 115 (198 115)
THE GAMBIA, AFRICA	Banjul	1 705 000	11 295 (4 361)
TOGO, AFRICA	Lomé	6 619 000	56 785 (21 925)
TRINIDAD AND TOBAGO, NORTH AMERICA	Port of Spain	1 339 000	5 130 (1 981)
TUNISIA, AFRICA	Tunis	10 272 000	164 150 (63 379)
TURKEY, ASIA/EUROPE	Ankara	74 816 000	779 452 (300 948)
TURKMENISTAN, ASIA	Ashgabat	5 110 000	488 100 (188 456)
UGANDA, AFRICA	Kampala	32 710 000	241 038 (93 065)
UKRAINE, EUROPE	Kiev	45 708 000	603 700 (233 090)
UNITED ARAB EMIRATES, ASIA	Abu Dhabi	4 599 000	77 700 (30 000)
UNITED KINGDOM, EUROPE	London	61 565 000	243 609 (94 058)
UNITED STATES OF AMERICA, NORTH AMERICA	Washington	314 659 000	9 826 635 (3 794 085)
URUGUAY, SOUTH AMERICA	Montevideo	3 361 000	176 215 (68 037)
UZBEKISTAN, ASIA	Tashkent	27 488 000	447 400 (172 742)
VENEZUELA, SOUTH AMERICA	Caracas	28 583 000	912 050 (352 144)
VIETNAM, ASIA	Hanoi	88 069 000	329 565 (127 246)
YEMEN, ASIA	San'a	23 580 000	527 968 (203 850)
ZAMBIA, AFRICA	Lusaka	12 935 000	752 614 (290 586)
ZIMBABWE, AFRICA	Harare	12 523 000	390 759 (150 873)

Games and Quizzes

Name the continents
Match the numbers on the map to the continent names listed.

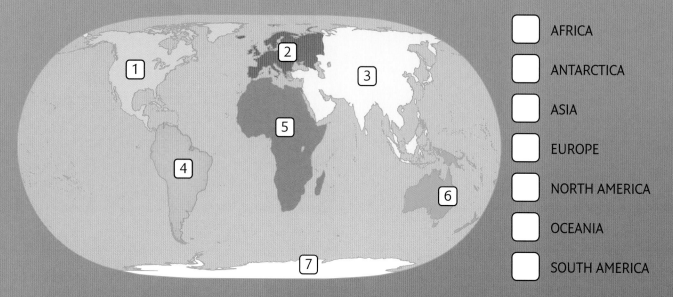

- [ ] AFRICA
- [ ] ANTARCTICA
- [ ] ASIA
- [ ] EUROPE
- [ ] NORTH AMERICA
- [ ] OCEANIA
- [ ] SOUTH AMERICA

Name the countries
Match the shapes to the country names listed.

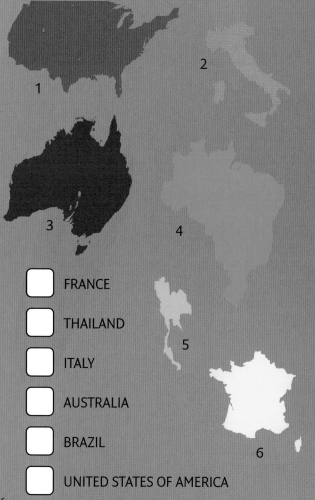

- [ ] FRANCE
- [ ] THAILAND
- [ ] ITALY
- [ ] AUSTRALIA
- [ ] BRAZIL
- [ ] UNITED STATES OF AMERICA

Search for cities
The 12 capital cities listed below are hidden in this grid. See how many you can find.

A	O	W	E	L	L	I	N	G	T	O	N
B	P	X	Z	P	O	J	X	Z	Q	J	O
W	A	S	H	I	N	G	T	O	N	V	T
X	R	K	Y	Y	D	W	V	J	F	X	T
C	I	K	P	F	O	X	Z	Q	J	F	A
A	S	Z	B	A	N	G	K	O	K	X	W
N	J	V	Q	Z	X	X	C	H	Z	Y	A
B	R	A	S	I	L	I	A	W	X	T	V
E	W	H	G	M	X	Z	I	Z	F	U	X
R	O	M	E	X	Q	V	R	J	Q	N	F
R	V	W	T	O	K	Y	O	V	W	I	Q
A	Q	W	H	G	M	X	T	J	V	S	Q

LONDON   WELLINGTON   CAIRO
PARIS   TOKYO   TUNIS
ROME   BANGKOK   OTTAWA
CANBERRA   BRASILIA   WASHINGTON

Quiz 1
1. What is the largest country in the world?

2. What is the capital of France?

3. What colour is the flag of Libya?

56

Colour match

All these symbols have a colour in part of their name. Find their correct name by matching a colour with one of the other words.

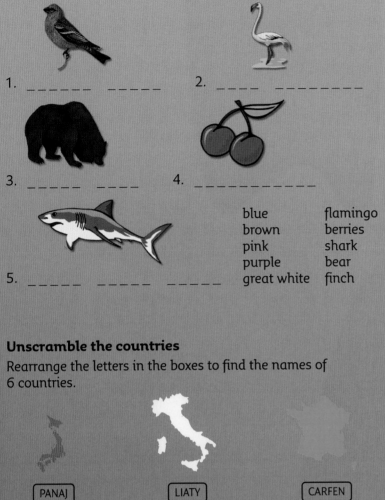

1. _ _ _ _ _ _ _   _ _ _ _ _

2. _ _ _ _   _ _ _ _ _ _ _ _

3. _ _ _ _ _   _ _ _ _

4. _ _ _ _ _ _ _ _ _ _ _

5. _ _ _ _ _   _ _ _ _   _ _ _ _ _

blue	flamingo
brown	berries
pink	shark
purple	bear
great white	finch

Unscramble the countries

Rearrange the letters in the boxes to find the names of 6 countries.

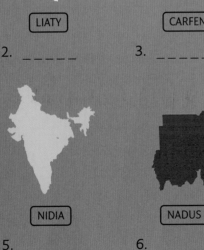

PANAJ
1. _ _ _ _ _

LIATY
2. _ _ _ _ _

CARFEN
3. _ _ _ _ _ _

XIECOM
4. _ _ _ _ _ _

NIDIA
5. _ _ _ _ _

NADUS
6. _ _ _ _ _

Quiz 2

1. What is the world's longest river?

2. How many colours are on the flag of Italy?

3. What kind of bears are found in Arctic regions?

Whose flag is this?

There are 16 country flags and 16 country names shown below. Try to match up the country names to their flag. Add the correct flag number to the box beside each country name.

1.
2.
3.
4.
5.
6.
7.
8.
9.
10.
11.
12.
13.
14.
15.
16.

☐ CHINA ☐ JAPAN

☐ CANADA ☐ GREECE

☐ PAKISTAN ☐ NEPAL

☐ BRAZIL ☐ SOMALIA

☐ CHILE ☐ SWEDEN

☐ AUSTRALIA ☐ KENYA

☐ NEW ZEALAND

☐ UNITED KINGDOM

☐ REPUBLIC OF SOUTH AFRICA

☐ UNITED STATES OF AMERICA

Answers on page 64.

Games and Quizzes

Name the oceans

Match the numbers on the map to the ocean names listed.

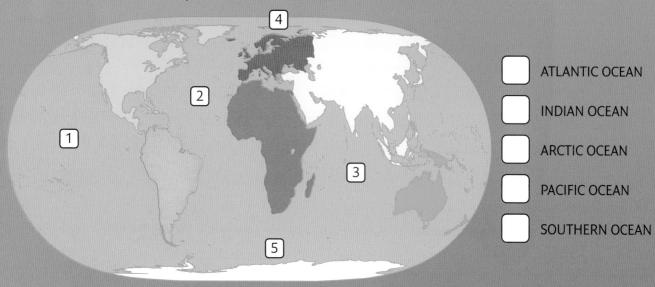

☐ ATLANTIC OCEAN

☐ INDIAN OCEAN

☐ ARCTIC OCEAN

☐ PACIFIC OCEAN

☐ SOUTHERN OCEAN

Name the symbol

Choose a suitable caption for each symbol from the names in the panel on the right.
Only one caption will match each symbol.

1. _____   2. _____

3. _____   4. _____

5. _____   6. _____

Puffin   Kiwi fruit   Owl

Bobcat

Polar bear

Grapes   Taj Mahal

Stonehenge   Hockey   Apple

Banana

Walrus   Cricket

Shamrock

Oil platform

Sydney Opera House

Quiz 3

1. What is the capital of Argentina?

2. How many blue stripes appear on the flag of Honduras?

3. In which country would you watch this sport?

Symbol Match

In which country would you expect to see these?
Add the correct symbol number to the box beside each country name.

1. Tower Bridge

2. Croissants

3. Liberty Bell

4. Taj Mahal

5. Kangaroo

6. Zulu house

☐ UNITED STATES OF AMERICA   ☐ FRANCE

☐ UNITED KINGDOM   ☐ SWAZILAND

☐ INDIA   ☐ AUSTRALIA

Which continent are you in?

Look at the groups of flags below.
Which continent would you be in if these flags were shown?

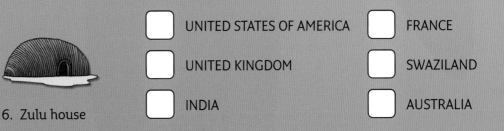

1.   2.

3.   4.

5.   6.

☐ ASIA   ☐ OCEANIA

☐ EUROPE   ☐ NORTH AMERICA

☐ SOUTH AMERICA   ☐ AFRICA

Search for countries

The 10 countries listed below
are hidden in this grid.
See how many you can find.

A	R	G	E	N	T	I	N	A	F	K	Y
N	V	G	F	Y	N	E	Z	U	Z	B	V
C	Y	D	Q	C	G	G	G	S	X	Q	J
H	U	N	G	A	R	Y	B	T	G	B	J
I	L	A	F	N	G	P	H	R	B	O	Q
N	N	L	Z	A	S	T	V	A	P	T	X
A	G	O	X	D	T	V	F	L	H	S	F
H	P	O	L	A	N	D	Z	I	H	W	F
H	Y	X	Q	Q	V	Z	X	A	Z	A	O
M	E	X	I	C	O	G	G	V	G	N	Q
Q	Z	J	B	Y	F	F	B	X	B	A	J
N	I	G	E	R	I	A	B	J	Q	K	P

ARGENTINA

AUSTRALIA

BOTSWANA

CANADA

CHINA

EGYPT

HUNGARY

MEXICO

NIGERIA

POLAND

Quiz 4

1. What is the world's highest mountain?

2. What is the capital of China?

3. In which country would you find these animals?

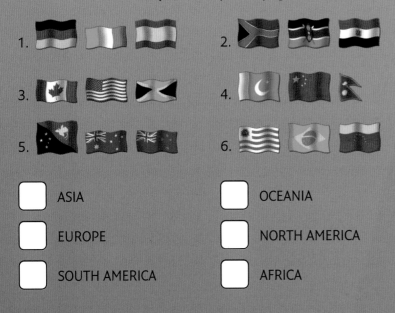

Answers on page 64.

Index

This index lists all the important place names shown on the maps. The grid code numbers and letters help you to find the correct position of the name on each map.

Answers

Try this!

2-3   GREENLAND

4-5   1. Canadian goose, Arctic tern, snowy owl, snow goose, ptarmigan
      2. Newfoundland, husky
      3. polar bear, musk ox, Arctic fox, wolf, brown bear, bobcat, caribou, moose, beaver, Arctic hare

6-7   1. blueberries, grapes, oranges, apples
      2. hotdog, hamburger, muffin
      3. peanut

8-9   1. tropical fish, sea horse, great white shark, elephant seal, monk seal, turtle
      2. parrot, toucan

10-11   1. Colombia, Chile   2. Bogota, Brasilia

12-13   1. emerald, diamond   2. anaconda

14-15   1. mackerel, sardine
        2. polo, skiing, football, motor racing

16-17   MADAGASCAR

18-19   1. camel, gerbil, baboon
        2. scorpion, tortoise
        3. hoopoe, hornbill bird, bee eater bird, secretary bird

20-21   1. grapes, oranges   2. cloves

22-23   1. Two. Germany and Belgium
        2. Greece   3. Norway

24-25   1. football, cricket, rugby
        2. yachting, windsurfing
        3. curling, skiing

26-27   1. Gouda   2. dairy cows, pigs, sheep
        3. croissant

30-31   Sri Lanka

32-33   1. reindeer, polar bear, Siberian tiger, Siberian husky, Siberian stag, brown bear, lynx, Caspian seal, lemming
        2. eider duck, snow goose, Ural owl

34-35   1. Arabian camel, Arabian fox, Arabian horse
        2. Mosque   3. cricket

36-37   1. tiger, snow leopard, Asiatic lion
        2. peacock, parakeet   3. Indian porcupine

38-39   1. Giant panda
        2. karate, sumo wrestling, skiing

40-41   1. surfing and scuba diving

42-43   FIJI   AUSTRALIA   NAURU

44-45   1. black swan
        2. sea horses, sperm whale, barracuda, flying fish, clown fish, great white shark, swordfish, octopus

46   1. ski plane   2. kayak
      3. snowmobile

Answers

Games and quizzes

Name the continents
1. North America
2. Europe
3. Asia
4. South America
5. Africa
6. Oceania
7. Antarctica

Name the countries
1. United States of America
2. Italy
3. Australia
4. Brazil
5. Thailand
6. France

Search for cities

A	O	W	E	L	L	I	N	G	T	O	N
B	P	X	Z	P	O	J	X	Z	Q	J	O
W	A	S	H	I	N	G	T	O	N	V	T
X	R	K	Y	Y	D	W	V	J	F	X	T
C	I	K	P	F	O	X	Z	Q	J	F	A
A	S	Z	B	A	N	G	K	O	K	X	W
N	J	V	Q	Z	X	X	C	H	Z	Y	A
B	R	A	S	I	L	I	A	W	X	T	V
E	W	H	G	M	X	Z	I	Z	F	U	X
R	O	M	E	X	Q	V	R	J	Q	N	F
R	V	W	T	O	K	Y	O	V	W	I	Q
A	Q	W	H	G	M	X	T	J	V	S	Q

Quiz 1
1. Russian Federation
2. Paris
3. Green

Colour match
1. purple finch
2. pink flamingo
3. brown bear
4. blueberries
5. great white shark

Unscramble the countries
1. Japan
2. Italy
3. France
4. Mexico
5. India
6. Sudan

Quiz 2
1. River Nile
2. 3 (green, white and red)
3. Polar bears

Whose flag is this?
1. Canada
2. Australia
3. Greece
4. United States of America
5. Pakistan
6. Sweden
7. Brazil
8. Kenya
9. China
10. United Kingdom
11. New Zealand
12. Japan
13. Nepal
14. Chile
15. Republic of South Africa
16. Somalia

Games and quizzes

Name the oceans
1. Pacific Ocean
2. Atlantic Ocean
3. Indian Ocean
4. Arctic Ocean
5. Southern Ocean

Name the symbol
1. Puffin
2. Kiwi fruit
3. Walrus
4. Sydney Opera House
5. Cricket
6. Stonehenge

Quiz 3
1. Buenos Aires
2. 2
3. Japan

Symbol match
1. United Kingdom
2. France
3. United States of America
4. India
5. Australia
6. Swaziland

Which continent are you in?
1. Europe
2. Africa
3. North America
4. Asia
5. Oceania
6. South America

Search for countries

A	R	G	E	N	T	I	N	A	F	K	Y
N	V	G	F	Y	N	E	Z	U	Z	B	V
C	Y	D	Q	C	G	G	G	S	X	Q	J
H	U	N	G	A	R	Y	B	T	G	B	J
I	L	A	F	N	G	P	H	R	B	O	Q
N	N	L	Z	A	S	T	V	A	P	T	X
A	G	O	X	D	T	V	F	L	H	S	F
H	P	O	L	A	N	D	Z	I	H	W	F
H	Y	X	Q	Q	V	Z	X	A	Z	A	O
M	E	X	I	C	O	G	G	V	G	N	Q
Q	Z	J	B	Y	F	F	B	X	B	A	J
N	I	G	E	R	I	A	B	J	Q	K	P

Quiz 4
1. Mount Everest
2. Beijing
3. Australia